ANCIENT ⊞ modern

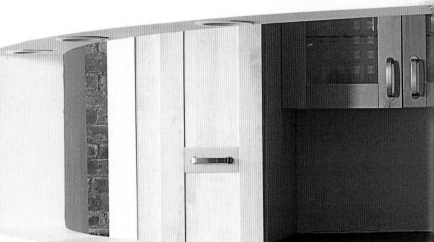

ANCIENT +modern

Cynthia Inions

Photography by Simon Upton

RODALE®

RODALE

WE INSPIRE AND ENABLE PEOPLE TO IMPROVE THEIR LIVES AND THE WORLD AROUND THEM

Text copyright © Cynthia Inions 2001
Photography, design and layout copyright © Jacqui Small 2001

First published in Great Britain by Jacqui Small,
an imprint of Aurum Press Ltd,
25 Bedford Avenue, London WC1B 3AT

Published in North America in 2001 by Rodale, Inc.,
33 E. Minor Street, Emmaus, PA 18098; www.rodale.com

Library of Congress Cataloging-in-Publication Data
Inions, Cynthia.
    Ancient + modern / Cynthia Inions.
        p. cm.
    Includes bibliographical references and index.
    ISBN 0–87596–936–4 (alk. paper)
    1. Interior decoration. 2. Interior architecture.
    I. Title: Ancient & modern. II. Title: Ancient plus
modern. III. Title: Ancient and modern. IV. Title.
    NK2115 .I47 2001
    747—dc21   2001002886

Printed in Hong Kong

Distributed in the book trade by St. Martin's
Press

    2 4 6 8 10 9 7 5 3 1 hardcover

CONTENTS

In the downtown New York studio of sculptor Elena Colombo, special attention is given to the importance of color, shape, light, and presentation. Placing a simple modern glass jar on top of an old dark wooden chest in front of a pale blue-painted brick wall creates a compelling composition.

INTRODUCTION

Combining ancient and modern—from constructing a twenty-first-century addition to a nineteenth-century townhouse to standing a modern oak table on an ancient kilim or fitting a stainless-steel sink in an old farmhouse kitchen—is an exciting and practical way to create a contemporary home.

Combining ancient and modern is not new. Throughout history, whether through inheritance or acquisition, people have adapted existing buildings and incorporated furniture and objects from previous generations and different cultures to create comfortable, individual—and at times fashionable—homes. At the beginning of the nineteenth century, simple and economic rural Scandinavian style embraced the influences of French decorative rococo and neoclassicism to create an original—and in time influential—look of its own. These additions did not displace what existed, partly because so much furniture was ingeniously built in to the simple wooden structures in which people lived, to optimize space. Swedish Gustavian style was characterized by signature combinations of the decorative and the plain, the grand and the simple, with natural textures, plain walls, and simple colors alongside checked or striped fabrics in red, blue, or yellow and white, gilded or decorative detailing, and painted wooden furniture.

Equally, there are historic precedents to the way many people choose to live now. Open-plan integrated interiors were common in medieval times; the ancient Romans preferred low-level relaxation on large floor cushions; and a modern Eames chaise longue is reminiscent of a Victorian one or even an ancient African daybed.

What is different about combining ancient and modern today, however, is a general freedom and confidence in our own sense of style, and a range of architectural opportunities to create original and individual living spaces. In the last ten years, the availability of an ever-increasing range of nondomestic spaces to convert into dwellings, and our access through media exposure to the work of imaginative and influential architects and designers, has had a massive impact on our perception of a contemporary home.

At the start of the twenty-first century, combining ancient and modern has also become important from an ecological point of view, since regenerating and reinventing existing buildings helps preserve precious resources. Examples include the conversion of industrial buildings into domestic dwellings, as in contemporary loft developments, and the restoration and modernization of historic homes, as in the revival of Victorian-Gothic wooden housing in San Francisco's Bay Area.

As this book shows, an ancient and modern aesthetic can be applied both in terms of architecture and in the creation of interiors. Adding dynamic contemporary extensions and architectural features to existing buildings; paring down historic homes to create simpler spaces; or combining antique and modern furniture, textiles, art, and artifacts in bold juxtapositions—these are all ways of creating individual and enjoyable spaces to live in. Ancient and modern can be combined in the very structure of a home or in the simplest of details, such as using antique teacups with a contemporary teapot when you serve tea.

The aim of this book is to present these different options by showing, describing, and celebrating a diverse range of inspiring interiors and ideas, all of which demonstrate the exciting new opportunities there are today for exploring ancient and modern combinations. Indeed, of the many homes featured, only three existed in anything like their present form ten years ago; most of the interiors photographed and described have been created much more recently. Five years ago, two former industrial buildings were either derelict or in the process of being restored and converted. One living and working space was a professional design studio; another was an office. A nineteenth-century house has been totally reorganized since the arrival of children. And an apartment in Paris has been transformed by replacing antique furniture with modern iconic designs. These spaces are now exciting ancient and modern environments, which acknowledge the architecture and function of the original buildings and provide contemporary homes that meet the different requirements of those who live in them.

Combining ancient and modern is a way of expressing our individual style. Where we live and the buildings we live in, how we organize and decorate our homes, and the furniture, textiles, art, and artifacts we surround ourselves with tell our stories. The material used for a floor, the color of a wall, the shape of a pot, the style of a chair, or the patina of a tabletop—all reveal our interests, passions, and cultural influences, and all add soul and texture to our homes.

OPPOSITE Traditional Japanese style is contrasted with bold contemporary architecture in this London loft-style apartment. The wall has a textured render, and the floor tiles are authentic riven slate. The space provides a dynamic backdrop for oriental antiques and artifacts.

CONCEPT

"To be modern is not a fashion, it is a state. It is necessary to understand history, and he who understands history knows how to find continuity between that which was, that which is, and that which will be." Le Corbusier

Putting together diverse ancient and modern elements, whether it is a contemporary metal table with nineteenth-century silver or an ancient Indian daybed on a white felt rug, brings out what is special and strong about them.

Any environment provides opportunities for combining ancient and modern, both in the structure of a building and the relationship between the structure and the elements within it. An attic apartment in Paris, for example, has nineteenth-century oak beams, wrought-iron window balustrades, and modern European furniture; the loft conversion of a former garment factory in New York combines matte concrete floors, white walls, and oriental antiques; and a conventional Victorian townhouse in London has a two-level glass extension at its rear.

Living in a space that combines ancient and modern is about coexistence and balance. Coexistence essentially means acknowledging our architectural heritage and finding ways to change or direct it into the kinds of spaces we want to live in. Balance is about incorporating compelling details from the past—whether they are the architectural features of a building or pieces of furniture, textiles, art, or artefacts—with our present and future requirements for our homes.

This chapter explains the terms "ancient" and "modern" in relation to creating a contemporary space and describes how the two concepts can be harnessed to create a powerful, enriching, and pleasing design. It examines the wide range of choices we have when it comes to selecting a place to live, and the different perspectives or starting points from which old and new might be brought together. It also outlines the key principles for combining ancient and modern—either to create striking juxtapositions that throw structures, elements, or objects into sharp relief, or to explore the connections between shapes and forms from widely different centuries and cultures.

Finally, the chapter introduces a theme that is central to the book: how a combined ancient and modern aesthetic enables us to create individual homes that reflect our diverse tastes and influences and tell our personal stories.

Contexts

The coexistence and balance of ancient and modern is an important theme in our cultural and day-to-day lives. Ancient forms and concepts are apparent in architecture, design, and fashion, from a dome or arch to a pair of denim jeans. Such forms appear as recurring templates. For example, the shapes and lack of ornamentation of nineteenth-century flatware is evident in the modern design classics of David Mellor. Or they can inspire reinvention, for instance a *stella*, or Roman magistrate's stool, was the inspiration for Mies van der Rohe's Barcelona chair, first produced in 1929.

An ancient and modern dynamic has been used in high-profile public buildings like the Tate Modern in London and the Louvre in Paris. For the Tate Modern, which opened at the beginning of the new millennium, architects Jacques Herzog and Pierre de Meuron reinvented a partly redundant industrial building to create a space for showing large-scale exhibits. The voluminous turbine hall of the original structure has been laid bare and acts as host to a series of interconnecting galleries. In Paris, the startling glass pyramid rising in the exact center of the Louvre is a symbol of creative bravado by architect Ieoh Ming Pei. The transparent structure, with fountains and three smaller pyramids in its court, underlines the symmetry of the former thirteenth-century palace.

In furniture design the purity and practicality of eighteenth- and nineteenth-century Shaker furniture is visible in many contemporary chairs, tables, and storage units. A 13-foot-long table made for a workshop in Cambridge, Massachusetts, is a typical example of ancient Shaker furniture, with a simple construction, tapering legs, and wheels to facilitate movement and cleaning. Similar simple worktables with wheels are today sold by retailers such as IKEA for use in contemporary flexible living spaces. In Japan, following the revolutionary deconstruction fashion of Rei Kawakubo of Comme Des Garcons, the fabric technology of Issey Miyake, and the inventive tailoring of Yohji Yamamoto, designs from a new generation that is looking to reconnect with ancient traditions include contemporary T-shirts with pockets made from fragments of antique silk kimonos.

All these cultural developments are inspiring examples of how old and new can be interpreted and combined. They demonstrate the strength and relevance of an ancient and modern aesthetic as a response to the big issues of the twenty-first century: finding a continuum between what exists and the future; making the best possible use of available and valuable resources; and—possibly the biggest issue of all—creating aesthetically and culturally rich environments.

RIGHT Slate tiles with an uneven surface provide authentic Japanese flooring in an oriental-inspired loft. Simple utility pieces like this antique footstool contrast with strident architecture to create a powerful ancient and modern environment.
OPPOSITE Contemporary details and fixtures, such as industrial steel windows and fin radiators, provide a high-specification setting for oriental furniture. The apartment, like Tate Modern seen through the window, is representative of the regeneration of former industrial buildings into vital contemporary spaces.

THIS PAGE In an imaginative conversion of a brick factory in New Jersey, an ancient hand-hewn African bed is juxtaposed with contemporary cost-efficient plywood flooring, which in turn contrasts with the nineteenth-century architecture.

OPPOSITE A mid-twentieth-century chair by Jean Prouvé, with an oak frame and a birch-veneered plywood seat and back, combines traditional carpentry with machine technology.

Defining ancient and modern

Exploring definitions of ancient and modern is an important part of our understanding and enjoyment of an ancient and modern aesthetic. This is not an academic endeavor; the aim of this book is to provide inspiration and ideas for combining two vital forces in contemporary culture. And while identifying examples of what is ancient and what is modern is a good way to acknowledge the differences between objects made centuries apart, it is also thrilling to discover similarities. A Georgian three-prong fork and an eighteenth-century Japanese footstool share a simplicity and practicality that makes them every bit as relevant and welcome in a contemporary space as a twenty-first-century chair by Marc Newson.

In the context of this book, "ancient" refers to buildings, furniture, and objects made before industrial machinery and production. A house with a basic frame made from

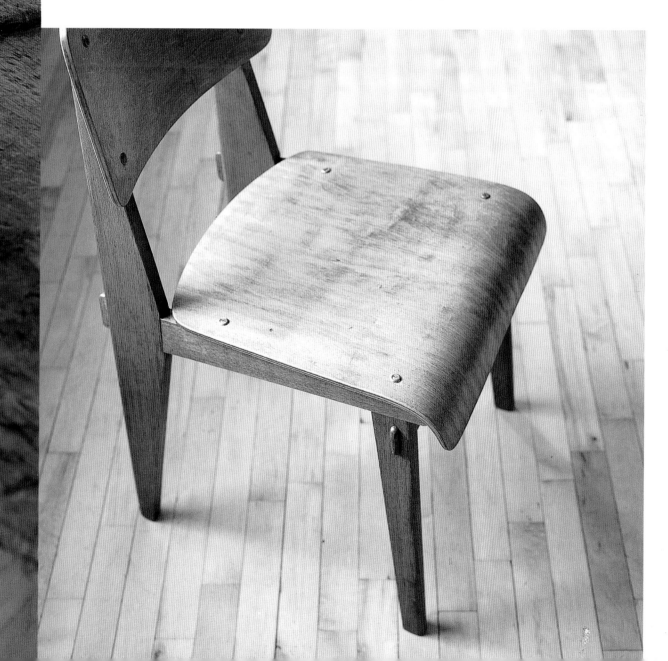

LEFT Antique utility items, like these pieces of flatware from the nineteenth century, add a sense of the past to a contemporary home in a direct and accessible way. Unlike ancient art and decorative items, they do not require presentation or display. **OPPOSITE** The unique shape and form of a contemporary ceramic by Rupert Spira contributes vitality, originality, and a contrast in texture and color to a sixteenth-century wooden shelf.

wooden joists and brick pillars—not steel and concrete—is an example. And although industrial manufacturing and mass-production techniques have largely replaced the making of building materials and furniture by hand, our heritage of expert craftsmanship and classic design is still a vital part of contemporary life. The structures that provide homes for many people, a competitive trade in every kind of antique from before the machine age—from architectural salvage to glassware—and a general passion for flea markets, secondhand stores, and grandparents' attics all bear testament to this.

The trace of humanity in the way ancient artifacts were made is an essential factor in their enduring popularity, but their patina of wear and use is equally central to their appeal in a contemporary home. An Early American cupboard with peeling paint, an eroded stone step or weatherbeaten brick wall in a converted schoolhouse, the darkened wood on the arms of a chair, or the random crisscrossing of marks on a copper bathtub—such traces of the past are visual and textural reminders of a previous existence and add layers of meaning and mystery to any surface. And perhaps we are also drawn to these handmade things, with their imperfections and the resonance and secrets they hold, because there is only a finite number of ancient buildings, pieces of furniture, art, and artifacts.

Whereas "ancient" can be defined relatively easily, "modern" is both a design direction and a perspective or way of seeing. In many ways, to be modern is to be of the moment, yet forward-looking. Yet, as this book illustrates, being modern can mean looking to the past as well as to the future. At the start of the twentieth century, however, "modern" was a clear-cut concept: It was a rejection of everything from previous centuries—styles like rococo, Gothic, and Empire. The beginning of the machine age, mass production, and the introduction of materials like tubular steel, bent plywood, and aluminum provide a logical division between ancient and modern architecture and design. In design terms, the machine age began around 1910, and within 20 years the concept of a contemporary home had changed significantly. By the 1930s and 1940s, appliances and consumer goods such as refrigerators and vacuum cleaners were commonplace throughout the United States and western Europe.

Yet this was not a period of single-minded progression in architecture and design. People like Le Corbusier, Alvar Aalto, Eileen Gray, Charlotte Perriand, and Jean Prouvé were producing diverse and inspiring work, developing signature styles, and gaining a following

among modern-thinking consumers. Meanwhile, however, the mass market remained fixed on traditional concepts and interiors.

During the twentieth century, design progressed from the radical visions of the Modernist Movement in the 1930s to the domestic retail revolution of Habitat with its colorful dispensable sofas in the 1960s and, finally, to the minimalist contemporary homes created at the end of the century. All were very different—and all were "modern." Designers and architects including Charles Eames, Frank Gehry, Arne Jacobsen, Mies van der Rohe, and Frank Lloyd Wright and minimalist architects like Tadao Ando, Luis Barragán, and John Pawson have set new standards and principles in modern design. And, like the duvet generation of the 1980s who gave up traditional bedlinen overnight in universal favor of big lightweight sacks of stuffing, once the concepts and ideas of these designers and architects were out in the open, they were assimilated for everyday use.

And while technology may have transformed our living spaces in many ways—from the low-maintenance, ecofriendly materials used to build contemporary homes to shopping on the Internet, watering our lawns by remote control, deflating plastic chairs to fit our body shape, and programming a lighting system to dim gradually while we eat supper—a modern lifestyle is not complex or inaccessible. A home that is essentially of the twenty-first century is instantly recognizable because of its informality, diversity, and freedom. It is possible to be modern, yet live in a nineteenth-century house with no central heating and few electric lights, or in a contemporary loft with secondhand sofas and junk-shop tables and chairs. Just as it is possible to be modern and live in a former brick factory with an eclectic mix of American and European twentieth-century furniture, or in a reinvention of an Arts and Crafts house with antiques from Rajasthan and industrial metal stairs. Individual and enjoyable combinations of furniture, objects, colors, and textures and a general sense of light and simplicity all contribute to the atmosphere of a modern space.

Being modern is about putting together different elements with regard to shape, form, and meaning and without regard to age, style, or origin. Seeing apparent similarities—for example in shape, form, and color—makes us look longer to seek out the differences, and this ultimately deepens our appreciation of ancient and modern. This book sets out to bring together inspiring examples of ancient and modern combinations—not as answers or formulas but as a celebration of individual stories and interpretations.

An ancient and modern aesthetic

An ancient and modern aesthetic influences the way a space looks and how it feels to live in. It is a way of evaluating and responding to a structure, a chair, or a door handle—whether they are ancient or modern—and will inform and direct your overall design concept for a building or room. An ancient and modern aesthetic can translate into a historic space with a capsule collection of iconic twentieth-century furniture, or a contemporary home with secondhand furniture found in junk shops or dumpsters. In either case, what you choose to leave out is just as important as the pieces you include.

However, creating an ancient and modern space is not about insensitively removing or obsessively obliterating architectural details in an effort to optimize light and openness, leaving only the bare structure itself to represent ancient. The essence of a place is in the moldings and door hinges as much as it is in large-scale structural elements like its facade. Although there may be a good reason for simplifying an interior by keeping only the minimum of original features—for example, you may want to reduce excessive decorative details or remove the walls to create an open-plan family area—it is important to be selective in what you take away and what you keep.

Nor is an ancient and modern aesthetic about preserving details simply because they are there, or totally restoring a building. Where is the vitality or energy in a space that does not change? Contemporary homes that work for the people who live in them evolve in response to changes in circumstances and new perspectives on lifestyle.

Architectural features are only one factor in an overall space. Furniture, textiles, lighting, art, and artifacts are equally essential and add an enlivening multilayering of shape, color, form, and historic or cultural references. However, it is important to use these elements selectively so that they coexist with and balance each other and their architectural surroundings. Creating clear and simple combinations of ancient and modern within a space, or in relation to the structure of a space, draws attention to the individual elements and to what connects them or makes them different.

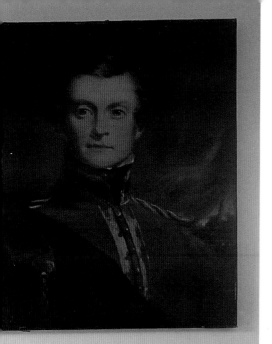

Ancient and modern perspectives

Developing a space with an ancient and modern aesthetic means acknowledging the scale and style of the original structure, considering its merits and potential, and creating a design that is sympathetic to the existing architecture and appropriate to individual requirements. This is true of any project, whether it involves converting a barn into a living/working space for an urban couple, designing a contemporary home for a family with a collection of antiques, or simplifying an interior as a backdrop to an eclectic mix of furniture and artifacts.

A direct way of implementing an ancient and modern aesthetic is to add or incorporate the opposite of what exists already—for example, to extend an ancient structure with a modern one; to refit a raw industrial space with slick, high-specification materials; or to introduce modern furniture into a historic house. This will create a powerful juxtaposition between different structures or between the structure of a building and the elements within it. However, a less direct response can provide opportunities for effective connections between existing and new structures and elements. For example, in a converted cowshed in Cornwall, England, the existing ancient building was extended with an identical structure and the whole was furnished with a collection of contemporary and antique furniture and art.

In architect John Pawson's conversion of a traditional wood-frame English barn, a few essential items of furniture offset the vast canopy of oak beams in the main living space. Every wall is painted white, and he has introduced new elements, such as a concrete floor throughout a series of interconnecting spaces, that are in keeping with the natural qualities of the structure. Pawson's reinvention focuses on an exhilarating sense of openness and creates an extraordinary contemporary environment.

In London, architect Pip Horne's custom-built house for the artist Anish Kapoor is a very different project. The structure is all new, with sculptural white walls spiraling through a central atrium, yet the artist's collection of heritage Indian icons and an eclectic mix of colorful and decorative antiquities transform the experience of being in the house. This is as powerful an example of an ancient and modern aesthetic as Pawson's barn, but is different in almost every aspect.

In a New York loft, an inexpensive way of transforming the structure of a space provides the key to a dynamic combination of ancient and modern. In fashion designer Han Feng's converted former factory, everything is the same color. This simplifies and unifies a network of pipes and girders and provides a plain backdrop to oriental antiques, voile banners, and brightly colored silk lanterns. This contrast between the structure of a space and the elements within it can be applied to many different settings.

The key principle of an ancient and modern aesthetic is to respond to the original structure and retain a sense of place. In Gert van de Keuken's Art Deco apartment in Paris, the structure has been laid bare with white walls and beige-painted concrete floors. This reduces a dominant architectural style to a simple backdrop with a sense of proportion and light. Classic twentieth-century furniture and junk-shop tables and chairs combine to create a welcoming and texturally rich space.

Architect Pierre d'Avoine's extension of a suburban London house centers on views and access to the outdoors. New openings in the existing structure and sliding glass doors at the back create long views through the house and a light, spacious living area.

Juxtaposition and connection

Different combinations of ancient and modern are based on the principles of juxtaposition and connection, and they radically alter and influence the way a space and everything within it is perceived. These principles can be applied whether you are arranging a cup and plate, putting together a collection of furniture, or exposing an original architectural feature in a building. Simple juxtapositions and connections of color, texture, and shape have a significant impact. Yet it is equally valid and workable to create historic and cultural combinations or your own esoteric theme.

Essentially, juxtaposition is a way of directing attention to differences between the structure and the elements in a space, or between the elements themselves. An example is the dining area in a conversion of a former nineteenth-century church in Yorkshire, which is furnished with a handmade wooden table and machine-made white Arne Jacobsen chairs. Connection is about finding and underlining links and common themes. For example, black-and-white photographic portraits from the early twentieth century could be displayed in plain white box frames.

Juxtaposition is a powerful dynamic. It is often through this that the true nature of a thing, whether it is a building or a fork, becomes apparent. Placing a round white bowl next to a rectangular black vase brings the different color and shape of each vessel into focus. Putting a round white bowl against a concrete wall or a block of color brings out, and draws attention to, individual surfaces and forms; it changes the way we see and experience both the bowl and the wall. Black and white, round and angular are bold and direct juxtapositions. Equally direct are textural contrasts—of rough and smooth, such as the natural surface of a bamboo table and the industrial polish of a stainless-steel bowl, or matte and glossy, such as flat-glazed walls and gloss-painted floors.

Presenting ancient or ethnic items in a contemporary setting isolates them from their usual cultural references and gives them impact and definition. For example, an African tribal doll in a pared-down Art Deco apartment, or an antique French chair with a gold frame and linen seat on a black-and-white vinyl floor are seen in a completely new way.

Ancient and modern juxtapositions translate effectively into architecture, furniture, art, artifacts, and everyday utilitarian fixtures and equipment. Place a mid-twentieth-century floor lamp alongside a Gothic stone fireplace set flat into a plain plaster wall, and the composition will project a visual sparkle that is profoundly different from the impact of either the lamp or fireplace alone. Insert an industrial-style staircase in a conventional Victorian house, or add a grandmother's collection of wooden spoons to a battery of stainless-steel kitchen

RIGHT This black-and-white combination is a dynamic juxtaposition of historic architecture and contemporary furniture design in the form of a 1950s Arne Jacobsen chair. The split wood of the walls and floors also makes a visual connection with the worn and cracked leather on the chair.

A+M

These ceramic bowls by Rupert Spira, on display in his sixteenth-century Shropshire farmhouse, illustrate basic principles of connection and juxtaposition and the way different backgrounds and surfaces affect the appearance of objects. Set against a black background, the black-and-white bowl appears predominantly white.

utensils, and time after time the power of these ancient and modern juxtapositions will strengthen and underline the shape, form, and meaning of the individual elements.

In structural terms there are many opportunities for juxtaposing ancient and modern. In a historic house, simply uncovering original floorboards to reveal a rich patina of wear will provide a textural contrast to anything with a hard edge—contemporary metal furniture, perhaps, or a concrete platform or steps. In industrial conversions the function and design of the original building is an alien context for contemporary furniture and fixtures. It is this that provides the opportunities for juxtaposition, and many conversions retain essential and authentic architectural details. Unfortunately, if key original features like metal windows or shutters have been removed, it is impossible to replace them.

Connection is an alternative way of combining elements in a space. It is used to create visual and textural harmony, for example, by grouping different kinds of chairs that are all made of beechwood or that originate in the 1950s. Beginning with two or three pieces (perhaps a dining table and chairs, which have a simple connection) that work well in a space is a good way to develop a capsule collection of furniture. In illustrator Max Gustafson's New York loft, most of the furniture comes from trips to neighborhood flea markets. Pale gray and blue rustic wood cabinets, all in a similar state of distress and wear, bare wooden tables and chairs, and basic country-style pottery combine harmoniously to add texture and natural shapes to an industrial environment. Creating a connection like this between different elements links them visually and groups them within an overall scheme so that no single piece dominates an environment.

Introducing color—either a single hue or a family of colors—is an effective way to create a sense of unity and simplicity. If you decide to use just one color, for example on walls, floors, and furniture, add texture and variation with different finishes. In an all-white scheme, a mix of glossy and flat paints and peeling patinas would add sensory and visual stimulation to a simple interior.

A family or palette of colors, whether they are based on historic colors found in original Shaker houses or are akin to those in Andy Warhol's Pop Art paintings, can be used to define different groups of elements while maintaining an overall harmony. For example, in a pared-down historic house, a palette of earthy browns connects 1930s leather sofas, European rustic tables, funky 1970s high-back

suede chairs, and ethnic wooden bowls from Africa. All these pieces are set against bare floorboards and white walls on all four levels—a simple structural space.

Look for compatibility and connections between shapes and forms. In the open-plan, pared-down Paris apartment of French interior designer Frederic Mechiche, imaginative connections are made between similar shapes and forms in ancient African artefacts, such as a tribal mask, and contemporary art photography, such as a modern portrait, set against a backdrop of antique white paneling and pale, bare floorboards. In Alastair Gordon and Barbara de Vries' converted brick factory in New Jersey, a French daybed in worn leather with a ticking mattress connects with an ancient African

bed made from a single piece of wood. Both items of furniture occupy central positions within different areas. The French daybed is on the ground floor, and the African bed is on the mezzanine level. And while it is difficult to see both pieces at the same time, one clearly echoes the other and the connection between them crosses centuries and cultures.

To make effective connections using functional items such as fixtures and hardware, focus on simple combinations like a Victorian rolltop bathtub with secondhand faucets in a contemporary bathroom, or a stainless-steel sink and laboratory faucets in an ancient kitchen. On a smaller scale, the pleasure of using a collection of ancient and modern storage jars or ceramic tableware and the

texture and patina that they bring to a contemporary home will override any mismatching of historic detail or style.

To create connections between structural elements such as floors, windows, and doors, take your lead from existing original features. Connections between materials work well—for example, installing new flat-panel oak doors in keeping with original oak parquet flooring, or laying a concrete floor next to an original stone floor. Be careful when using architectural salvage from a very different environment than yours: Antique doors from India require a lot of plain space to look good. Also, installing a wide variety of elements out of their original context can lead to a jumble of references that will distract from the sense of connection.

RIGHT With its plain, functional design, this Georgian glass is oblivious to changing styles. Its classic outline and simple shape set the standard for contemporary glassware. **OPPOSITE** The parallels in simplicity and construction between this antique wooden country-style table and contemporary metal chair connect across centuries.

Ancient and modern motifs

The shape and form of many contemporary products, usually everyday tools like spoons, cooking pots, baskets, and faucets, have not changed over centuries. Although in some cases the way they are manufactured has altered beyond recognition—spoons that were once made individually by hand are now mass-produced by machines—their basic form, or template, remains the same. Equally, many current handmade products and crafts, such as a bent-plank stool or a ceramic bowl, are versions of ancient templates. This is most clearly seen in traditional products and designs. For example, in architectural firm Ushida Findlay's loft conversion in London's Bankside development, handmade Japanese shoji screens in wood and paper provide lightweight space dividers without blocking light or reducing the structure's flexibility and sense of openness—precisely how shoji screens have always been used.

This African workstool succeeds on a functional as well as an aesthetic level. It is lightweight and portable, and it encourages the sitter to keep a straight back with feet on the ground and weight evenly distributed. With its simplicity and graphic outline, it is ancient and yet modern.

The simple poetry and precision of this clay teapot with a bamboo handle was created by refining and simplifying a basic design through generations. Its smooth surface and simple shape make it perfect for holding in both hands. When the pot is in use, the clay keeps the tea hot, and the bamboo handle stays cool for carrying and pouring.

The visual appearance of a table knife—its color, patina, and shape—is a vital part of its appeal in a contemporary home. Yet it is also important to consider how it feels to use: its weight and balance in the hand, the smoothness and length of the handle, and the sharpness of the blade. These plain utilitarian knives work well in an eclectic table setting.

tique glassware and flatware, with everyday contemporary items,
oosing simple, undecorated shapes and forms.

This hand-wrought metal cross is ancient African money. The size of an adult's hand and the weight of a small chicken, it is as much a powerful symbol of wealth as a practical means of exchanging or transferring it. The cross is also remarkably modern and sculptural in its form.

The utilitarian style of this spoon originated in the nineteenth century—a combination of the traditional skills of English silversmiths and the flamboyant style of Huguenot artisans. The advent of industrial production and a general climate for setting design standards in everything from buildings to tablespoons made it possible to buy multiples of this simple design.

Inexpensive ethnic cooking utensils, like the oriental ladle and African wooden spoon, provide a hands-on connection with ancient traditional crafts and resourceful low-tech design. The joint between the scoop and handle expands to a tight fit when the utensil is in use.

A personal space

Few people are content to inherit a previous occupant's interpretation of a space, let alone ideas and configurations from 50 years ago. We all seek to reinvent what we inherit or where we live. An ancient and modern aesthetic is a way of incorporating history and heritage in a contemporary environment without being nostalgic. It offers an opportunity to make the best use of existing options and strengthens our ability to conceptualize alternatives.

By liberating us from conventional values that place greater importance on things we know to be expensive antiques or good investments, an ancient and modern aesthetic enables us to celebrate architectural features and other elements in a space for their own sake. A flea-market plate can contribute as much visual delight to a table setting as an antique candelabra. In the same way, it is possible to arrange a living room around a simple window with a pleasant view rather than a historically important Gothic marble fireplace, or to stand a contemporary painting in front of the fireplace to take it out of the space altogether.

Family treasures, hand-me-downs, and objects of personal significance can be included in a space without compromising the overall scheme or the objects themselves. Alternatively, such items can be presented or contained in a way that is in keeping with a specific style. For example, an antique wooden cabinet can be integrated into a contemporary white apartment by painting a wall or section of wall mellow gray to support the piece of furniture and reduce any conflict between the elements.

It is in our nature to avoid exclusivity and look to many different sources for emotional, aesthetic, and even spiritual stimulation and fulfillment. Therefore it is logical and appropriate to bring together disparate elements or objects to create an inspirational and enjoyable place to live. For example, a New York loft belonging to an English and American couple has a mix of European antique furniture, contemporary American art, and ethnic textiles from India, Morocco, and Turkey. An ancient and modern aesthetic is a positive approach to creating a home that is a true reflection of our individual style.

While it is good to plan and consider options, it is best to avoid being obsessive or over-academic about specific historic details or design icons. Trust yourself and your instincts about how you want to live. It is often the accidental or expedient decision—perhaps choosing to do something because it is quick and inexpensive rather than the best way of furthering a grand scheme—that enhances a space beyond expectation.

By themselves, the elements and objects in this New York loft, which include a flea-market lampstand and china, a table made out of new wood, and aluminum chairs, would appear low-key and commonplace. However, bringing them together creates an individual and engaging ancient and modern space.

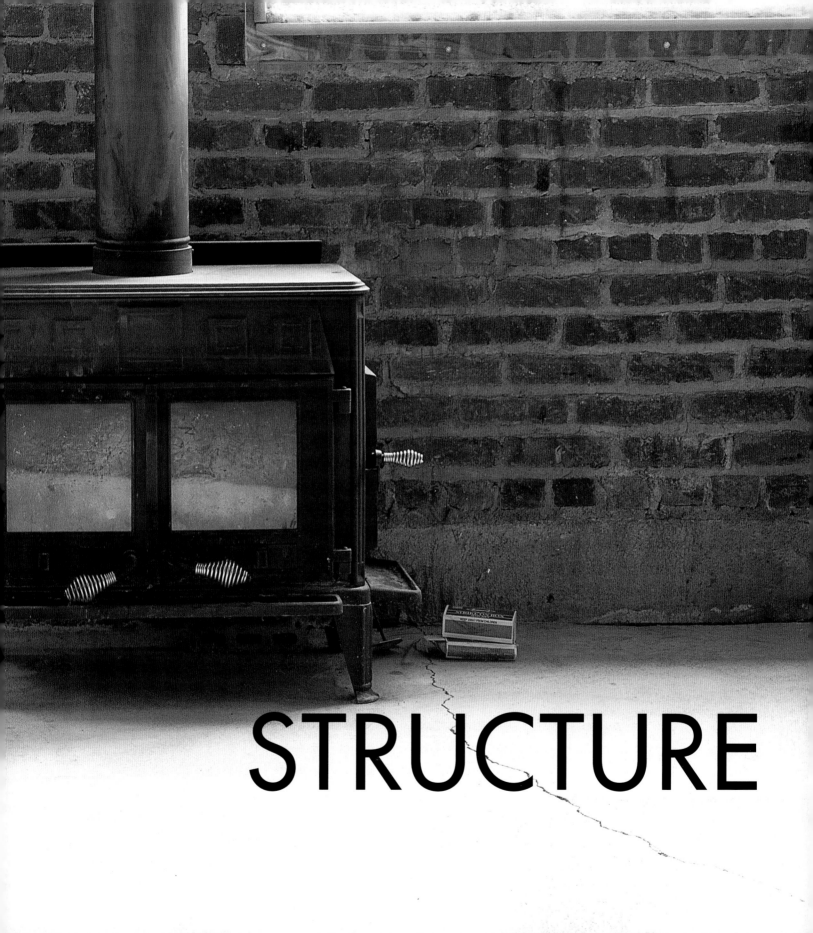

STRUCTURE

> **"A good space
> will accommodate
> an Empire chair
> every bit as well as
> a Corbusier chaise."**
> Doris Saatchi

THIS PAGE The structure of this open-plan New York studio is new, apart from the antique Moroccan doors leading to a bedroom. Recently added to the top of an existing building, the space has high-ceiling construction with glass walls at each end. **PREVIOUS PAGES** The ancient and modern architectural solution for this converted brick factory in New Jersey included exposing the structure of the space and using materials such as concrete, raw wood, and steel.

Altering an existing structure in any way, from remodeling the internal architecture to simply repainting it, offers many opportunities to reinvent your home, add to the enjoyment of living in a space, and combine ancient and modern.

From large-scale projects such as dismantling and reworking the interior of a conventional townhouse or converting a former factory to an open-plan loft space, to smaller projects like refurbishing a rural cabin or simply exposing and repairing an original floor, there are many imaginative and resourceful ideas to inspire and encourage us to undertake structural projects of our own.

If there is a current movement or direction in making a contemporary home, it is a movement against uniformity and design-by-formula. The perfect-white-box ideal, for example, can work brilliantly in some circumstances—usually as a solution for uncompromising minimalists with big budgets—but this approach can diminish the individuality of a place and flatten out its meaning. The alternative, working with what exists and not a preconception of an end result, is a celebration of the experience of a place.

Acknowledging the original function and design of a building as a positive asset and incorporating or interpreting this in any structural changes or plans to regenerate or update a space demonstrates an enjoyment of juxtaposition that is an essential aspect of an ancient and modern aesthetic.

The ideas and solutions presented in this chapter demonstrate how to combine ancient and modern in a way that celebrates and uses the original structural elements of a building. A selection of different examples illustrates how to adapt or incorporate original architectural features in a positive and dynamic way so that they do not predetermine an overall design aesthetic. For example, a sculptural custom-designed contemporary house can accommodate an enriching collection of heritage furniture, artifacts, and textiles in a series of bold juxtapositions. Equally, it is possible to repair the original structure of a Federal townhouse and create a light, welcoming, comfortable contemporary environment that avoids any sense that the past is simply being recreated as an exercise in historical correctness.

RIGHT Bare floorboards and white walls, ceilings, and window frames simplify and update the structure of this eighteenth-century townhouse in east London, and provide a pared-down environment for flea-market furniture and art.
OPPOSITE The curving wall in this converted spice warehouse in New York is an imaginative architectural feature that separates a kitchen from eating and relaxing areas in an open-plan space.

New living spaces

Ten years ago, the age and style of a building's exterior was a good indication of the configuration of the space and overall aesthetic within it. This is definitely no longer the case. Just as for all kinds of social, economic, and cultural reasons there is no typical family unit and no typical working day, there is no longer any easy way of categorizing a home. Architectural terms like "open-plan," "multifunctioning," and "integration of indoor and outdoor space" apply equally to such diverse properties as a 1960s apartment, a Victorian brownstone, or an expansive industrial conversion.

Essentially, the place you live in was either built as a dwelling of some kind or is a conversion from a nondomestic space. Examples of domestic architecture such as historic houses, modern developments in period or contemporary style, apartments, and, increasingly, custom-designed houses on any suitable site with proper zoning are all recognizable fixtures in every rural and urban landscape in the Western world. And while most domestic architecture consists of convenient, practical structures whose design and proportions are familiar, if conventional, it also offers excellent potential to create individual contemporary homes.

There are many different ways to adapt and update existing domestic architecture. In addition to dismantling what exists and reinventing domestic space, it is possible to transform a structure

Setting up a relaxing area between a row of big windows and classical-style support columns in this New York loft acknowledges the positive and original structure of the space and makes good use of available light. A wall of bookshelves with window insets creates an appealing light-well effect.

beyond recognition with simple and inexpensive modifications. And while domestic properties still make up the biggest proportion of housing options, conversions of nondomestic buildings are providing more and more places to live. These include former factories, railroad depots, schools, offices, and old churches. The fact that the buildings appear on the market in the first place reveals a lot about important changes in our communities—urban regeneration, downsizing of commercial premises, and the increase in working from home that has been made possible by computers. Often in central urban locations, buildings like these offer the potential to develop alternative living spaces that are very different, both externally and internally, to those provided by conventional domestic architecture.

In addition to introducing a whole new concept and understanding of what a contemporary home can look like, conversions are exerting a powerful influence on domestic architecture in general. The new vocabulary and expectation of space, light, openness, and even industrial fixtures is spilling over into conventional buildings. (Loft-style is so popular that some new developments are built to look like former industrial spaces and claim to offer this type of accommodation.) With such diversity in the housing market, it is impossible to apply any kind of preset design formula. Certainly, a conventional apartment or house is very different from an industrial conversion, yet both have positive original assets.

Assessing your space

If you are contemplating any structural changes, begin with a comprehensive assessment of your options and yourself. Big issues to think about are how to make the most of the space in your home, cost efficiency, and how the changes will improve the quality of your life.

An essential part of this assessment is information about yourself and the people you live with. Whether you live with one other person or a group of individuals or are part of a family, it is important to take everyone's requirements into account. This is basic building-block information and will indicate how best to organize space and areas for change or improvement. If you have children, think about their possible future requirements. For example, include in your plans the option to create a space for them, away from parents or other family members, as they grow older and more independent.

Look at your home objectively and note any positive or negative features. Find out about the age and origin of the building. This will help you appreciate the configuration of its space and the materials it was built from. Are there any fixtures or architectural features that are specific to the structure? Draw a plan and note the general layout and positions of facilities and utilities. Look at the way you use the overall space and how it facilitates—or possibly limits—the way you live. Think about the different rooms in terms of their size, quality of light, and where they are, and decide which functions they are best suited for. Map out the routes people take when they move from one part of the building to another and note any inconvenient restrictions or points of congestion.

Getting the basic structure and layout right is worth time and effort, although structural solutions are not always without compromise. For example, it may be necessary to specify wooden window frames in place of metal ones to keep within budget. Plan to get the framework right and then specify the best materials you can afford.

It is equally important to consider how any changes you make will affect the essence of the building. For example, in Langlands and Bell's low-key update of a historic house in London, or Alastair Gordon and Barbara de Vries' conversion of an industrial space in New Jersey, both solutions are a response to the essential character of a building. Simplifying and reducing a structure will often achieve this without taking away the authenticity of a place.

Once the framework of the building is right, you can create the ambience you want by adding furniture and details like a rug or a textile, or by painting a wall.

Changing the structure

To see the potential for change in your home, take an overview and think of it as a unit that defines an amount of space and contains an amount of light. Each unit is built from a combination of walls, floors, ceilings, and windows in a variety of materials such as concrete, wood, glass, stone, metal, and brick. Its shape is usually determined by where it is built: It may stand alone on its own site, in a line or row, or in a stack or block with other units of the same or varying size.

The volume of space within each unit is usually rigid or set. Sometimes it is possible to add space by extending sideways, upward, or downward. For example, when buying the top floor of an office building in east London to convert it into an apartment, designer Fiona Naylor also bought "air rights," or permission to add another level to the existing structure. The roof extension is a glass and metal construction in contrast to the heavy-duty 1950s light-industrial architecture below. With views across London and an outside play area for her children, the extension is like a massive light box and transforms the whole space.

It is sometimes possible to use previously unusable space, for example, by converting a basement or the attic space under a roof. If these areas do not have enough height for day-to-day use, a basement is a useful storage or laundry area and a roof space converts to an ideal sleeping platform. However, even without extending an existing structure, it is possible to manipulate and optimize the perception and experience of space.

The level of light within a unit is dependent on light coming in and circulating effectively. Note where it enters and how it moves around throughout the day. Is the space light and airy? Is it possible to add extra windows or skylights, or take out or reduce a wall that is blocking light? Any area with good light is welcoming —ideal for a key activity like relaxing, eating, or working.

Basic standards and controls apply to all levels of structural change, so it is essential to follow regulations. Always contact the relevant planning and engineering departments in your municipality before making alterations. Also check utilities and service systems, which are often subject to controls. Know where water pipes and electricity cables run and avoid or reroute them if possible.

Finding out about any restrictions or regulations that concern the building you live in will give a good indication of the scope of possibilities. For example, it may be impossible to alter the design of a window in a nineteenth-century house for reasons of historic preservation. If a building is listed as being of special architectural interest, it is important to obtain permission before making structural alterations to the interior. In a twentieth-century building with multiple occupancy, you may not be allowed to remove a concrete staircase because of fire regulations. However, it is sometimes possible to negotiate a solution or an alternative plan.

Conservation and zoning regulations can restrict the extent to which changes can be made to the street-facing facades of buildings to make sure that they remain architecturally compatible with adjacent ones. However, there is often greater freedom to change the rear of a property, away from the general view. If this is the case, it may be possible to totally remodel a structure behind a street-facing facade.

If you plan to adapt or restructure a building, or if you are looking for a property to work on, get professional help. A good architect's skills include spatial awareness, experience, and the ability to see a job through to completion with a proper plan of action. He or she will also have the vision to assess the potential as well as the reality of a property. Engineers, surveyors, and planners offer expertise and advice in all technical matters. If you plan to introduce openings or internal windows, add mezzanine levels, or remove part of a floor, the structure of the building may require further support and strengthening by inserting an additional beam. The strength of the beam will depend on the weight it will have to bear or how many floors there are above it.

Some nondomestic conversions can tolerate extensive alterations without additional strengthening. This is because of the industrial standards and specifications of the original construction. For example, when the architectural firm Fernlund and Logan converted two floors of an industrial building in New York, it was possible to create a double-height living area without additional supports.

Possible options for structural changes include radical alterations, a fusion of what exists with something new, and low-key simplification and rationalization.

LEFT Converting this sixteenth-century barn into a studio workspace required low-key changes to the original structure, such as cementing glass panels into ventilation slots in the original stone wall. **OPPOSITE** Using architectural salvage, including a staircase and paneling from a nineteenth-century building, designer Frederic Mechiche has reworked the layout of his Paris apartment.

In his radical redesign of the interior of a four-bedroom house built at the beginning of the twentieth century, architect J. F. Delsalle has removed every original structural element to create a contemporary open-plan environment with a powerful sense of space and light.

Radical alterations

The radical option is about extreme restructuring—dismantling or rejecting most of what exists to reinvent a very different environment. In architect Richard Rogers' well-known conversion and amalgamation of two row houses in London, the facade of the building is all that remains of the original structure. Inside his family home, the main living area is a magnificent space with a double-height ceiling that extends across the width of two houses. Daylight circulates without the obstruction of the former walls and floors, and as a result the sense of light and space within the building is extraordinary.

Where Richard Rogers subverts the concept of a conventional house with fantastic dimensions and uncustomary views within the space, architect John Pawson's conversion of a modest period townhouse—also in a London location—follows a pattern that is typical of many similar buildings, with a kitchen and dining area in the basement, a living room on the ground floor, main sleeping and bathing areas on the second floor, and children's bedrooms on the top floor. However, his radical restructuring behind the original facade includes a dynamic staircase that spans two levels in a single diagonal line and liberates valuable living space. An industrial-standard steel frame supports stone floors on every level and a stone bathtub next to the main bedroom.

In both properties the juxtaposition between original and modern architecture is direct. Although their facades give no clue to the restructuring within, domestic buildings that date from a very different era than ours have been effectively adapted to provide original environments for contemporary families.

With conventional homes the challenge is often how to reorder a traditional layout of rooms to create greater openness and integration. With nondomestic conversions it is often the exact opposite. The challenge is how to divide space without detracting from a sense of openness, without obstructing light and preventing it from penetrating into the middle of the space, and without imposing an inappropriate domestic layout.

In the conversion by Fernlund and Logan mentioned on page 42, the solution was to maximize daylight by replacing the original factory windows with a glass wall and then to arrange activities around it. The main living area is a double-height space on the first level with magnificent views, thanks to this feature. The sleeping and bathing areas range around the central well from a gallery on the second level.

In architect Nik Randall's conversion of a former Victorian schoolhouse in London, contemporary mezzanines with open-tread staircases fit within the original structure like single freestanding constructions. There are junctions and juxtapositions where these and the original structure connect. The mezzanine levels sit on metal beams that in turn are set on the original oak beams, but these junctions are kept to a minimum. Where the floor of the sleeping-mezzanine level joins the original structure, a border of glass underlines both the separation and the connection between the two.

Introducing galleries or mezzanines and removing parts of floors are radical architectural changes and are relevant to all kinds of structures. Whether you take on an existing domestic space and adapt it or convert a nondomestic unit, imaginative design and planning can create a dynamic new environment. However, a project of this kind requires vision, commitment, determination—and a big budget. It is less expensive to custom-design and build a new house than radically restructure an existing one of a similar size.

The fusion of old and new

The fusion option is less radical. It is about finding ways to work within an existing structure, or extend part of it, in order to modernize or customize existing space. These include adding an extension, replacing a staircase, taking away or cutting back solid walls, inserting a skylight, or introducing sliding partitions.

Architectural firm Azman Owens' reinterpretation of a modest Victorian row house in London took the existing layout of the rooms as a starting point. Most of the original walls remain in place to define different living areas. The changes the architects made, such as inserting internal windows and widening doorways, add to an overall sense of openness and connection within the space. A contemporary extension in the rear garden has a glass roof and seems open to the sky. It provides a direct contrast to the original structure, which has a welcoming sense of enclosure.

Azman Owens' use of high-specification materials like glass and stone alongside original floorboards and weather-beaten brickwork is a solution that offers a powerful juxtaposition of ancient and modern elements. Recycling or salvaging architectural materials and fixtures is an alternative option that is appropriate to historically correct restorations. A cow shed in southwestern England, converted by architect Jonathan Ball and Hugh Lander, a historic building adviser, is an example of this type of project. Historically and geographically correct roof slates and stone from a local abandoned building were used in the restoration of the original structure and in a new extension that adjoins the cow shed at right angles.

The original building is now split into two levels, with two bedrooms and a bathroom on the lower level and a third bedroom, shower room, and gallery area on the one above. The extension forms a double-height open-plan living space for cooking, eating, and relaxing. Ingeniously, the new walls comprise a layer of inexpensive breeze blocks behind a layer of authentic stone. They provide good insulation and mimic the depth and resonance of the original walls, so the new window and door recesses appear equal to the original ones.

An example of less conventional yet no less ingenious recycling is the conversion of what had been a commercial space in midtown Manhattan by the architectural firm Lot/ek. A single structural device intersects the space diagonally, and effectively separates living and working areas. The device is the aluminum siding of a container truck, cut into different sections that pivot, rotate, or open upward to reveal a compact kitchen and shower and provide access to a sleeping area. A wooden frame supports the siding, yet the effect is of a truck sliding through a building. The installation is in keeping with the raw industrial fixtures, which include concrete floors and surface piping, and is inventive, functional, and strangely poetic. The art of this kind of juxtaposition is to bring out the essence of a place, and its success is often dependent upon the clarity and texture of the original structure. In this case the bold, raw state of the original building was equal to the boldness of the architectural device, so neither dominates the space.

Wherever you live, refine and edit the original structure to present a simple single message—an authentic sense of place. Whatever you take away will strengthen what remains.

A freestanding wooden platform on support struts bolted to a new concrete floor makes a bold addition to the conversion of a nineteenth-century brick factory, without altering or connecting with the original structure of the building.

 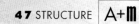

THIS PAGE Reducing the amount of furniture and objects in a space and unifying floors, walls, and ceilings with color, as in this early twentieth-century wooden house on Long Island, both simplifies an interior and brings the architecture into focus.

OPPOSITE The original architectural features in this 1920s Paris studio include a double-height window and internal terrace overlooking the main living and working area. Painting the walls and ceiling white enhances the sense of space and light and gives greater clarity to elements and objects.

Low-key changes

While reduction is vital for the fusion process, it is also an important part of making low-key changes. This option is about simplifying an environment and reducing it to what is essential. Even without removing any structural features, it is possible to manipulate what exists by reorganizing it—eliminating excessive furniture and clutter will go a long way to redefining a sense of place—or using color to present it in a different way.

The use of a single paint color unifies and simplifies a space as well as updates it. In designer Ann Shore's former Georgian home in east London, every surface apart from the bare floorboards is plain white. Shore chose not to restore the original paneling or replace a missing fireplace, preferring the simple effectiveness of paint to unify odd sections of brickwork or baseboards. Since the house is inherently austere, white optimizes light and a sense of space. It also provides an excellent backdrop to a juxtaposition of mid-twentieth-century furniture and ethnic artifacts. Despite a lack of obvious conveniences such as central heating, Shore's home expresses an unquestionably modern spirit.

As in Shore's house, white maximizes an overall sense of light and space. Deep colors like black or inky blue blur boundaries and distances between walls, ceilings, and floors. Lilac, pale green, and anything neutral produces a mellow welcoming effect. Bright, crisp colors like yellow, sky blue, or mint green often intensify a sense of being enclosed and work well in moderation.

In addition to simplifying a structure and diminishing obtrusive decorative elements, color can highlight special features and add definition. For example, an ornate ceiling in blood red or regal purple can be dynamic in a plain white space. Most colors look good in a block, but intense ones like bright orange or graphite work exceptionally well, creating a dramatic change of pace. A bright color will draw attention to an element in a room, for example, if it is painted on the wall around an original fireplace. Or it will direct attention away from a feature if it is used on the wall opposite it. Using different colors throughout a home can indicate changing activities: soothing blues, greens, and lilacs for sleeping and bathing, and livelier lemon or lime for cooking and eating.

Walls and doors

External walls and doors can outline whole cities, streets, and buildings. A facade may be subject to controls and restrictions that prohibit radical alterations, so frontage frequently remains true to the original design. However, architectural changes to an existing structure can be successful at the back of a building. Replacing a solid brick wall in a former factory with glass sliding doors or adding a concrete box to a Victorian row house are examples.

Internal walls are essentially devices for division and separation, and doors provide access to a room or space. It is possible to remove or modify internal walls without subverting the qualities that attracted you to the building in the first place, although alterations like these are not always cost-efficient. If you plan to reduce or take away a structural wall, it will be necessary to insert a steel, concrete, or wooden beam to take the weight of the floors above it. Even extending a doorway or an opening to the full height of the wall may mean that additional support is required. If a wall conceals electrical wiring or water pipes, these services will have to be rerouted, making the project more complex. If you add a wall, possibly to subdivide a spacious loft, it can incorporate essential services—for example, power and water supplies to a kitchen or bathing area—and provide built-in storage.

Some changes, such as removing part of a wall or replacing it with a glass panel, widening a doorway, or simply taking away the door will make better use of existing space and optimize daylight. They will also add internal views and help to unify the interior. Alternatively, if you do not want to make structural changes or if they are prohibited by zoning regulations, using light colors, reflective finishes, and plain roll-up shades will maximize the existing space and light in a low-key way.

Walls and doors do not have to be fixed in one place or follow conventional gridlike divisions of space. In a loft in downtown Manhattan, a floor-to-ceiling panel set diagonally across one corner of a room, with access on either side, conceals a work area from the living space. Oblong windows cut into the panel allow light to enter from each side.

Movable walls are ingenious functional devices and come in a variety of forms that include rotating, pivoting, sliding, or folding sections in steel, wood, plastic, or sandblasted glass—even a nylon sheet with a zipper. Their big advantage is that they are flexible and give you the freedom to change and manipulate the overall space on a day-to-day basis or to adapt to changing circumstances. For example, a movable wall can be used to reveal and conceal a work area in a living/working environment, or to create an optional sleeping area in an open-plan space.

Laying bare original surfaces by exposing brickwork or wooden doors and paneling, or by stripping wallpaper down to bare walls, provides context and texture for a domestic space and a juxtaposition with modern structural elements like glass or stainless-steel panels. In the ancient and modern apartment of architecture professor Nigel Coates, the wooden doors were partially stripped to reveal layers of different paint colors and present a capsule history of decoration from the nineteenth century.

ABOVE A 500-piece bamboo wall links different areas in an open-plan London loft. Although not based on a traditional Japanese design, it adds contrasting texture, color, and form to a Japanese-inspired interior. OPPOSITE This dynamic curving wall contrasts with the original architecture of the space and divides a kitchen area from a living area. A geometric cutaway allows connecting views.

The big advantage of sliding walls and screens is that they are flexible. Shoji screens, which are fundamental to traditional Japanese interiors, are used in this open-plan London loft to make an enclosure for dining or sleeping. They also provide optional separation between the main sleeping and living areas.

A doorway can be a major architectural feature or provide a low-key transition between rooms. This doorway in a New York loft is a focal point of the space, with a low-level opening and ancient decorative wooden doors in a double-height white wall. It leads into a bedroom and connecting bathroom decorated with a Moroccan theme.

Internal doors and walls delineate the proportions and logic of a space and, depending on the materials they are made from, indicate whether a room or area is private or public. These vast metal and glass doors suggest openness and connection even when they are closed, whereas the wooden doors beyond do not.

ors determine how different areas are connected or separated. For example, glass
nnection, whereas solid ones provide complete separation.

The laid-bare structure of this barn on the grounds of ceramicist Rupert Spira's sixteenth-century farmhouse in Shropshire, England, is now a studio/workshop. Part of the original structure has been divided into a separate room by creating a wall of horizontal planks. The main crossbeam is original.

The raw structure of this brick factory in New Jersey, with an exposed brick wall and industrial-size windows, is a key reason for living in this space. Restoring and exposing every structural element, pouring a new concrete floor, and installing a wood-burning stove all help to domesticate the space in a way that is in keeping with the original character of the building.

Installing eighteenth-century salvaged wood paneling in this Paris apartment changes the configuration of the rooms and the position of the doors. Painting the paneling with flat white paint unifies it without covering up cracks in the wood and provides a compelling contrast with modern classic twentieth-century furniture.

RIGHT Adding an extra
skylight on one side of
the roof of this artist's
studio brings in extra
light without radically
altering the structure of
the historic building.
OPPOSITE In this
conversion of an 1820s
church, simple gauze
drapes focus attention
on the shape and size
of the impressive arch
windows without the
distraction of a view.

Windows

Daylight is fundamental to our well-being and enlivens everything from plain white walls to a ceramic pot. However, the architectural style of a building determines the level of light within it, and it is not always possible—or desirable—to alter this. For example, small windows in a period cottage are characteristic of the style of the building, whereas large windows are typical of loft-style conversions. The level of incoming light and sense of openness to the world outside is very different in each space. It is important to find ways to work with an existing structure, orienting space to take advantage of daylight moving through it and balancing a sense of openness with a sense of enclosure and seclusion. Before altering existing windows or adding extra ones, consider how any changes will affect the space and your use of it.

In general, big window areas create light, welcoming spaces to live in, so add windows and make existing ones bigger if you can and if it is appropriate to your requirements and the style of the building. Solutions that will have a low impact on its structure are most likely to get zoning approval. Even if front-facing windows are beyond repair, planners may stipulate that you replace them with copies rather than change their style, in order to preserve the original facade. You are more likely to get planning approval for alterations to the rear of a building. Here you may be able to do something radical or ingenious with windows or sections of glass, either using them as a continuation of the existing architectural style or as a contrast to it. Adding a glass-and-concrete extension,

replacing a section of wall with a glass panel, or increasing the ratio of glass to frame in an existing window will have a positive impact by increasing the amount of daylight in your home.

Inserting a skylight in a flat or sloping roof creates a luminous well and is ideal for brightening the space in the core of a building or bringing light into one like a church or factory that was not originally designed as a home. A skylight above an existing stairwell in a remodeled roof-space or in the middle of a large space with windows at each end creates a beam of light that will transform anything directly below it. Introducing any new source of daylight this way can initiate a total reappraisal of a space by turning a previously unappealing low-light area into a dynamic and welcoming one.

Consider windows as integral to the structure of a building and keep them plain. In a Federal-style house, painting the windows, shutters, and wooden paneling pale gray unites and simplifies the structural elements in a room and draws attention to its proportions, creating a sense of order and space. Even an imposing bay window will become less dominant if the frame is painted the same color as the walls and ceiling. In a pared-down interior, any architectural style or size of window, such as steel-pivot windows in an industrial space or even a decorative round window in the conversion of a former church, will benefit from simple presentation and create a bold juxtaposition of ancient structural elements with a contemporary environment.

FROM LEFT TO RIGHT

The original floorboards in this early twentieth-century beach house come under heavy use from wet and sandy feet. Paint is a low-maintenance option for updating, recoloring, and protecting them.

In this eighteenth-century priest's house in Yorkshire, England, a pared-down aesthetic focuses attention on structural elements like an archway, wide door, and natural stone floor in the main hall.

Reworking an interior is an opportunity to juxtapose flooring materials. Here, stone slabs in a hall lead into dark hardwood planks in a general living area, underlining the different uses of the space.

Inserting borders or patterns into a floor by using a contrasting material, such as these mosaic tiles in concrete, can enliven an expanse of uniform flooring.

Traditional Japanese tatami mats introduce a soft, natural texture to an area. In this oriental-inspired space, they also provide an alternative base for a futon.

In this New York loft, underfloor heating transforms a concrete floor into a comfortable area for low-level relaxing on a horseshoe arrangement of cushions.

Exposing original floorboards in ancient buildings can reveal appealing inconsistencies, like the misaligned floorboards in this nineteenth-century house.

Floors

A floor is integral not just to the structure of a space but to its look and feel. Essentially floors provide a base to any given level, separate multiple levels, and sometimes separate different functional areas. The flooring material can provide a harmonious base to unite all other elements or be used to create juxtapositions with the style of architecture and furniture. The textures and colors of different materials transmit a whole range of visual and sensory messages that influence our perception and enjoyment of a place. For example, an expanse of concrete with underfloor heating is no less cocooning in its own way than a wool carpet, but it suggests a very different use of space. Hard and structural, it directs attention to the quality of light or openness in a space and draws a bold line under any furniture, object, or work of art. A carpet, by comparison, is a soft furnishing that brings the entire floor into use as a place to sit or lie on in comfort.

The key options for floors are to expose and possibly repair an original one, to install an alternative (perhaps on top of the original), or to introduce a floor covering.

Exposing an original stone, wood, or concrete floor is a way to acknowledge an authentic detail. Concrete as a backdrop to American country furniture, for example, will provide a powerful juxtaposition of ancient and modern elements. If an original floor requires extensive repair, it is possible to make this a feature by using contrasting new and old materials, such as bright plastic putty to plug holes in worn wooden boards, or concrete to replace missing slate tiles.

Replacing a floor or installing a new one provides an opportunity to manipulate the impact of different materials on existing architecture. Salvaged floorboards in a contemporary interior, or plywood sheets cut into oversize blocks in a traditional one, are cost-efficient solutions. Glass flooring on a mezzanine level will allow light to penetrate to the area below. Other options include concrete, stone, slate, marble, brick, stainless steel, and ceramic or quarry tiles. Some materials, like stone and glass, are best left in a raw state. Wood and concrete are receptive to different finishes, such as flat or glossy varnish, paint, or resin.

Floor coverings include cork, linoleum, coir, rubber, seagrass, and carpet. Any of these options provides opportunities for juxtaposition or connection with the structure of a space, or can help to simplify or update it in preparation for ancient and modern furniture and details.

If insulation against noise and loss of heat is a priority—this applies especially in apartments—it is possible to inject or insert buffer materials into structural cavities or raise a wooden floor on rubber pads. These installations are becoming less expensive and are worth investigating as an alternative to wall-to-wall carpeting. As a low-tech solution, inserting either string or wood pulp and glue in the gaps between floorboards will reduce noise and heat loss.

Finally, a note of caution. Changing an existing floor is disruptive and represents a major investment. It is important to consider the impact different options will have on the structure, appearance, and overall feel of your home. It is also essential to think about any changes you may wish to make in the future and choose a type of floor that will be flexible enough to work with these.

Stairs

A staircase is the spine of a building and provides essential connection between different levels. How it looks and relates to other structural elements, how it divides and uses space, how it links different levels, how it affects light, and even how it sounds when you walk on it are all factors that will contribute to the aesthetic of your home.

As with any original feature, it is important to review what exists before making alterations. With a period staircase, the right decision is often to leave it alone. (If it is of special historic or architectural interest, building regulations may prevent you from changing it.) In this case, integrating a staircase into a general living area—fire regulations permitting—by removing internal walls or widening a doorway gives visual and physical access to an important architectural feature and provides a dramatic focus in a laid-bare space.

Check an old staircase for safety and repair it if necessary. However, it is often counterproductive and not cost-efficient to undertake a full good-as-new restoration. Worn wooden stair treads and banisters or layer upon layer of paint provide clues to years of use and add an individuality that would be diminished if the stairs were restored. If you opt to paint them, possibly to integrate them with an overall color scheme, use rubber paint or several coats of floor paint with a durable varnish to even out any minor fractures in the wood and combat splinters or nail heads. Wax the original wooden handrails as a contrast to the color. An alternative to painting the stairs is to cover the treads with neutral flooring like linoleum or rubber tiles.

If you plan to install a new staircase, possibly because the original one is beyond repair or you need to access new levels, think about the visual impact as well as the safety aspects of different options. For example, an industrial steel-mesh staircase is a dynamic architectural feature, either in a loft-style apartment or in contrast to a conventional domestic interior, and allows light to penetrate to the space beneath. Even basic metal treads and a tubular steel handrail put together with scaffolding hardware can be every bit as impressive as a traditional design in oak.

BELOW LEFT A standard-issue industrial staircase using cost-efficient tubular steel and open metal treads provides a dynamic contrast to the architectural style of this early-twentieth-century family house and its decorative ancient and modern furniture.
BELOW RIGHT The design and construction of this Gothic staircase in a remodeled church make it a dominant feature. (Unusually, the stairs lead to the former chapel.) Keeping the rest of the area plain and light balances the historic architectural feature.

Integrating a staircase into a general living area by removing internal walls or widening a doorway gives visual and physical access to an important architectural feature.

This sweeping wood and wrought-iron staircase in a Paris apartment is a piece of architectural salvage. Its elegant form and light, worn treads connect with the shape of the Barcelona chair and the patina of its worn leather.

Architectural features

Features such as fireplaces, window and door moldings, ceiling molding, wood paneling, and wrought-iron balustrades chronicle the design, construction, and evolution of a building. They provide a link to a particular period or to the building's original use, and their relevance to an ancient and modern environment is to add context and a sense of place.

However, it is essential to find a balance between past and present to avoid overwhelming a space with excessive detail and history. Emphasizing a single, simple feature sometimes has far more resonance than leaving everything in place. In a loft apartment, keeping only the industrial steel loading-bay doors provides a reminder of what the structure was used for and adds texture and contrast.

Original features can be diminished by insensitive conversions. For example, the impact of an ornate ceiling is reduced by the insertion of a partition wall. Removing the wall will restore the ceiling as a feature and reinstate a sense of proportion to the space.

Consider the condition of features when deciding which to retain and which to remove or replace. For example, if a section of decorative coving is in less than perfect condition, do you remove it, restore it, or leave it as it is? Coving often conceals gaps in the plaster where the walls meet the ceiling, so removing it would involve covering or filling them in. Copying and restoring it could be expensive, although in a building of historic interest, regulations sometimes require this. So leaving the coving as it is may well be the solution. However, giving a bold or decorative feature unnecessary prominence can undermine the unity of a pared-down environment.

It can be difficult to be objective about what to keep and repair because of the values we give to our architectural heritage. Yet values change, and it is best to assess features in terms of how they fit in with a contemporary style. A modest wood-frame-and-brick cottage with an open fireplace and stone hearth is now a premium space precisely because of its original construction and plain architectural features. On the other hand, a grand feature like a Victorian Gothic built-in oak bookcase, which once stood for wealth and social importance, is of much less value today and could be given less prominence by painting it the same color as the walls.

Creating a space with an ancient and modern aesthetic will help you make decisions about all the structural elements in your home and direct you toward a total concept that reflects your own style.

ABOVE LEFT A wraparound white space with white walls and ceilings and terrazzo flooring contribute to the visual impact of this restored marble fireplace in an 1860 New York house. ABOVE RIGHT A low-key fire surround with inset blue-gray slate tiles and giant Scottish beach pebbles is the focus of this bathroom, which has a Japanese-style cedarwood bathtub. The colors and materials combine to create a mellow, natural environment. OPPOSITE Set flat into bare pink plaster walls, this architectural salvage Gothic stone fireplace is one of a pair in an open-plan living area. A contemporary glitter painting hangs on the wall between them.

Industrial conversion

A CONTEMPORARY REWORKING OF A NINETEENTH-CENTURY BRICK FACTORY

LEFT The wooden mezzanine is supported by raw-looking diagonal wooden struts held together with locally made metal brackets. This low-tech installation is freestanding within the original walls and connects with the concrete floor for rigidity. **BELOW LEFT** The low-tech staircase is made out of aluminum T-bars with ash treads. Its open design optimizes the sense of connection between different levels without blocking light. **MAIN PICTURE** The area underneath the 10-foot-high installation is an open-plan living space. The kitchen area consists of stainless-steel fixtures and appliances, which provide a contrast to the original brickwork.

A former brick factory in New Jersey, built in 1894, is now the family home of Alastair Gordon, Barbara de Vries, and their children. With the input of friends and architects Henry Smith-Miller and Laurie Hawkinson, the couple took on a dilapidated building and began a 3-year project of restoration and conversion.

Despite its industrial origins and plain construction, the factory is a handsome building. Its imposing shape, size, and orientation and the proportion and position of its windows suggest a classical style of architecture. The biggest challenge in converting the space was turning it into a home without losing sight or sense of the original structure. The solution was to install bold contemporary architectural

structures in the interior and leave the brick exterior and windows intact. The living space at the heart of the building is now ingeniously divided on two levels: the ground floor and a wooden mezzanine. The architecture and construction of the mezzanine is deliberately raw and temporary-looking, to fuse with the bare brick walls and concrete floor of the space. Yet this simple division has been the key to transforming a vast area designed to house industrial equipment into an individual home compatible with the requirements of a professional creative couple and their young family.

The building is entered through a grand glass-and-metal doorway that leads directly into a large workshop/studio. This remains in a relatively raw state and may be developed in the future. A wall of semitransparent sliding plastic panels divides the overall space in half, with the workshop/studio on one side and a spacious open-plan living area on the other.

Introducing the mezzanine provided a logical division to the open-plan space, with an integrated area for cooking, eating, and relaxing on the ground floor, and sleeping, bathing, and working areas above. The mezzanine is a 10-foot-high platform made from wooden crossbeams with plywood panels for flooring, surrounded by a wooden rail and a transparent screen made from bulletproof plastic—all inexpensive industrial materials. The whole structure is supported on struts bolted to the concrete floor with aluminum footings.

The general living space underneath the platform includes a children's area, an interconnecting bathroom, and a separate office behind permanent divisions, but in essence the ground floor is open-plan. The kitchen consists of low-level industrial shelving units between a stove, dishwasher, and stainless-steel sink unit. The work surface is blue stone, and a stainless-steel backsplash runs the length of the kitchen area with additional open shelving. In keeping with the structure of the building, this is a good-looking, hard-working area with no decoration or excessive detailing. It demonstrates the confident and resourceful fusion of ancient and modern throughout the space.

It was essential to create separate spaces on the mezzanine, specifically for the adults' and children's sleeping areas and the bathroom. Installing a combination of stationary and sliding plywood panels to divide the area without losing a sense of space was an inexpensive and low-impact solution.

All the architectural features and materials in this imaginative project are cost-efficient and resourceful, and the mezzanine is the most obvious example of this approach. There are many other examples of inventive design. The lightweight plastic panels that divide the main workshop/studio and living spaces are one of the key structural elements, providing insulation and separation without blocking essential light. On the mezzanine level, identical panels attached to a beam effectively screen an office. The staircase to the mezzanine level is made of aluminum T-bars with ash steps, and the roof insulation is hidden with yards of iridescent fireproof material.

Like everything else in this exceptional space, the mix of furniture and objects reflects an appreciation of both basic low-cost solutions and unique investment pieces. Contemporary aluminum clip-on spotlights hanging from the mezzanine, an ancient African daybed, and a set of Windsor chairs designed in the 1950s are good examples.

BELOW The upper level is predominantly a family space for sleeping, bathing, playing, and relaxing. Sliding plywood panels, hanging from a wooden frame, provide optional divisions and enclosure.
OPPOSITE LEFT AND BELOW RIGHT Well-chosen fixtures in the bathing area, including a child-friendly sink, look too good to conceal, so the sliding panel stays open when not in use. Two well-placed mirrors reflect light and extend the space with views of ancient and modern architectural juxtapositions.
OPPOSITE ABOVE RIGHT Semitransparent plastic panels attached to a beam provide a low-tech division between an office and general family space. The panels blur the visual impact of office equipment and storage without blocking essential light from the inner areas.

Modernization and connection

RESTRUCTURING AN EDWARDIAN ARTIST'S STUDIO AND A GEORGIAN COTTAGE

BELOW This view shows the roof of the Edwardian studio on the right and the Georgian cottage in the background.
RIGHT Taken inside the former studio at ground level, this photograph shows the cooking and dining areas. The front door of the cottage is at the end of the passage on the left.

This imaginative and radical architectural transformation updates two modest historic buildings in London and joins them to make a single dynamic contemporary space. The project by the architectural firm Stickland Coombe involved gutting, remodeling, and refurbishing the studio and cottage, increasing the incoming light and introducing high-specification materials to unify the structure and create an area for living and working. While the structure within is now radically modern, the street-facing facades of the two buildings remain the same.

In the Edwardian studio, which was rented by Charles Rennie Mackintosh between 1915 and 1928, a monolithic blank white wall is a dynamic focal point, both in the main living area and in the overall space. As an architectural feature, it hangs from the original roof of the studio and

The studio is now an expansive living and entertaining space. A new skylight in the roof brings light into the barnlike structure. The owner collects contemporary art, and the monolithic wall above the fireplace is used for film screenings.

The architects' radical scheme works with the original shape and historic context of the buildings.

OPPOSITE This view shows the interior of the cottage, looking toward the former studio. The passage leading into the main living area is lined with cabinets for essential storage. The stairs on the left lead to a mezzanine work area.
ABOVE LEFT A traditionally shaped bathtub with plain feet and faucet presents a dynamic profile, visible from the bed, that makes no concession to historic style.
ABOVE CENTER A new staircase leads down to the main hall, and French doors provide access to a compact roof terrace.
ABOVE RIGHT The upper level of the cottage now comprises open-plan sleeping and bathing areas. A change of color compounds the change in scale from the living and working area downstairs and adds to the sense of enclosure and privacy.

magnifies and celebrates its asymmetrical apex. As a practical device, it conceals storage for glassware and entertainment equipment, houses a flue for a contemporary gas-log fire, and provides a permanent blank screen for film projection.

Opposite the wall, looking toward the cottage, the apex of the roof forms part of a geometric jigsaw of cutaways and openings. On the ground level, the cutaway and opening on the right are part of the kitchen area. The opening on the left leads out toward the cottage and main entrance. The cutaway triangle on the upper level is a mezzanine work area with a built-in work table and storage.

The level of light in the studio, which houses a collection of photographs and contemporary paintings by British artists, was an important consideration, so a new skylight was added and existing ones were modified. The skylights also illuminate the blank wall and create shadows on either side.

A wide hall leading from the original front door of the cottage to the studio beyond forms a bold link between the two buildings and provides full-length front-to-back views of the space. A circular skylight is a luminous architectural feature in the center and adds a dynamic geometric shape to a series of openings and cutaways —access to the entire interior radiates from this point. The main living area is directly ahead. The axis of the hall and a sense of space and light ahead work together to draw you into this impressive open-plan

area. A row of ten identical doors lining the wall on the right conceals central heating and a hot-water tank, and a comprehensive storage system. To the left there is a separate bedroom and shower room and the stairs to a mezzanine working area. This has views over the main living space. To the right there is a reading room and new stairs to the upper level of the cottage.

The traditional Georgian cottage, which originally had a central staircase, retains a sense of enclosure in contrast to the openness of the studio and provides a logical environment for bedrooms and a reading room. There are two separate rooms on the ground level, while the upper level is now a spacious interconnecting bedroom and bathroom with access to a roof terrace.

Despite this open-plan arrangement, the upper-level space is in complete contrast to the main living and working area in terms of size, simplicity, and color. Moving the stairs and making the area open-plan were relatively simple structural changes. The prominent architectural feature is a storage unit that separates the bathroom and stairs.

The challenge was to combine two very different structures—Georgian and Edwardian—with very different original functions—domestic building and artist's studio—to make a coherent and enjoyable contemporary space to live and work in. The architects' radical scheme works with the original shape and historic context of the buildings to create a spacious, light, and welcoming home.

Simplification

REINVENTING AN EIGHTEENTH-CENTURY TOWNHOUSE

From the outside, this modest townhouse is unprepossessing. The only indication of the sensitive reworking within it is the historic gray paint on the original frames of the sash windows.

Built in 1790 in the East End of London, the Georgian house is on four levels, including a basement and a roof space. The owners, artists Ben Langlands and Nikki Bell, were drawn to it because both the house and the neighborhood are rich in history and culture, so it was essential that any alterations did not detract from the building's origins. The house is tall and narrow—a quarter of the width is taken up with stairs and hallways screened by a single wall of Georgian paneling that runs the full height of the structure—so

ABOVE LEFT A former doctor's examination couch with cut-down legs and a linen-covered mattress makes a snug reading area on the ground floor.
ABOVE RIGHT The original plain eighteenth-century paneling screens the hall and stairs on every level. Apart from the exhibition space on the second floor, the paneling is waxed and provides a warm soft backdrop to every room.
OPPOSITE The all-white scheme on the second floor provides a permanent exhibition space for the artists' work, which includes monochrome installations like these chairs.

FUNCTION

"Taking the simple approach allows scope for self-expression and for creating an environment which will continue to work and give pleasure."
Sir Terence Conran

THIS PAGE Efficient planning, which makes the most of space and natural light, creates a practical, welcoming environment for combinations of ancient and modern. In this kitchen, stainless-steel storage cabinets and white kitchen units are contrasted with a pickled oak floor and antique table and chairs.
PREVIOUS PAGES Installing sliding shoji screens in a traditional Japanese-style tatami room provides optional separation within an open-plan loft space.

A contemporary home is both a sanctuary and the environment in which we relax, cook, eat, sleep, bathe, and possibly work. If you have children, it is also where they will play and explore the world around them as they grow up.

Organizing a home so that it functions efficiently on a day-to-day basis therefore involves making practical, cost-efficient, and ergonomic decisions about such issues as the kind of work surface that is right for a kitchen, how to provide enough storage in a living room, and where to position a single chair and an adjustable light for reading. Yet how an interior looks and feels is equally important to our enjoyment and well-being: A plaster wall painted a pale color will enhance a feeling of space, while the worn texture of an antique country table will bring warmth to a streamlined modern kitchen. Acknowledging a sense of place and balancing this acknowledgment with the requirements of contemporary life is the key principle of an ancient and modern aesthetic. Basing your decisions on this principle will allow you to create a functional space that is individual to you and enjoyable to live in.

Practical decisions about where different functions and activities take place within a home depend on individual requirements and preferences. However, the logic of a building's architectural style and original features often suggests how the space could be used and presents powerful reasons for a certain kind of organization. When you assess the potential function of a room or area, its proportions, the level of daylight within it, its position in relation to the overall space, and any significant decorative features like a fireplace or ornate ceiling are all important factors to consider. Conventional concepts about how to organize space also influence our decisions. Examples are sleeping on an upper floor rather than in a basement or close to a living area, bathing in a separate room, and socializing or relaxing in the largest and most important space—one that often has architectural features like original paneling, a fireplace, or big windows.

This chapter describes how a wide range of ancient and modern elements, from furniture to kitchen appliances, floor coverings to existing architectural features, can be combined to create spaces that are suited to specific functions and uses.

Relaxing

An impression of softness and a sense of sanctuary are essential elements in a relaxing area. Softness doesn't just mean soft furniture to sit or lie on; it means creating a cumulative effect with paint colors, floor coverings, furniture, textiles, lighting, and accessories. Combine white walls and pale original floorboards in a nineteenth-century house with contemporary furniture and ancient ethnic artifacts and textiles, for example. Or use middle tones like gray or pewter for walls, with dark brown or black flooring and an eclectic mix of contemporary artifacts and predominantly ancient furniture. Soft rugs or carpets, ambient lighting, and possibly curtains or blinds to modify incoming daylight and provide privacy all contribute to a welcoming environment. Even if you sit on a hard chair at a table, lie in the bathtub watching television, or read in bed more often than you sit on a sofa or in an easy chair, creating a personal haven is a positive step toward achieving a relaxed and enjoyable lifestyle.

Relaxing areas are conventionally where people meet and socialize. In domestic buildings living rooms are often bigger, lighter, and grander than other areas, with finer finishes and architectural detailing to underline their importance. In an industrial conversion, large windows or original structural features like the brick wall in a former Victorian factory often indicate the best location for an area to relax in.

Consider how you want to define a relaxing area and what its focal point will be. An antique fireplace or a modern wood stove is a traditional and logical option. If an interior lacks features like these, use art objects, a painting, textiles, or a block of color on a wall to provide a focus within the space.

The next step is to plan how to orient a mixture of ancient and modern elements like chairs, tables, and lamps into a compatible and harmonious arrangement. Begin with the largest piece of furniture, perhaps a modern sofa or an antique cabinet for storing entertainment equipment. If there is more than one large element, find a balance between them and take account of any prominent architectural features. For example, in a living room with an original fireplace, a traditional chesterfield sofa could be positioned to face the fireplace and a modern low-level teak and steel cabinet could be placed against a wall on one side of it. Experiment until you create a feeling of balance and order. Consider movement and access around any key elements—especially if room or cabinet doors open into an area—and how well the arrangement responds to different-size groups of people, for example, a couple or a gathering of friends using the area. This indicates where to place smaller items such as easy chairs and occasional tables and lamps.

ABOVE The design and central position of the metal staircase, in front of a dynamic wall of windows giving spectacular views of New York, indicates that this low-level relaxing area is of key importance in a studio space.
OPPOSITE This built-in bookcase contains and imposes order on a collection of books without detracting from the welcoming informality of the area. Graphic contemporary uplights on the support pillar provide atmospheric lighting at night.

Big windows with a big view of the
River Thames and the London skyline
provided a logical starting point for
orienting and organizing this expansive
loft space. The oriental sofa and chairs,
set in a traditional arrangement around
a low table, are appropriately generous
and bold in size, shape, and color, and
work well in this contemporary
environment.

If an interior is open-plan, or if you want to use a space for more than one purpose—eating or working as well as relaxing, for example —create divisions with lighting, textiles, hangings, or floor coverings, or position furniture so that it defines an area. In the conversion of a former upholstery workshop in London's East End, an Arts and Crafts table with a display of magnificent ethnic figures and masks demarcates a relaxing area within an open-plan space. In a former spice warehouse in New York, a contemporary modular sofa defines an L-shaped relaxing area, and in an artist's Art Deco studio in Paris, an arrangement of two 1950s Bertoia lounging chairs with sheepskin cushions and a low table and footstool with an ancient animal skin underfoot effectively communicates intimacy and relaxation within an open-plan space.

A relaxing area is a multifunction space for activities like listening to music and reading, so storage and display space is needed for a wide range of items including stereo components, CDs, videos or DVDs, books, and magazines. Ancient and modern storage options include built-in and freestanding items. A period house might have original built-in shelves and cabinets. Alternatively, explore contemporary options such as white, wall-mounted low-level cabinets, which add an architectural feature and provide display space for ceramics or photographic prints. Freestanding storage options include modern low-level teak cabinets in a historic house or apartment, or an antique French armoire in a loft conversion.

Keeping everything in one place and possibly out of view, for example by using an antique country cupboard with peeling paint for audiovisual equipment, CDs, and videos, will diminish the impact of technology on an interior. Antique armoires provide excellent storage options because they are deep enough to accommodate televisions and stereo equipment, new shelving can be inserted for maximum efficiency, and they add an ancient feature in contrast to, or in connection with, other elements.

When you put anything into an area, always work with prominent architectural features like decorative ceiling molding, wooden paneling, a central motif on the floor, or an obvious symmetry in the position of doors or the alignment of windows. Disjunctions and asymmetry create visual tensions that can have a negative impact. For example, placing an armoire off-center against the wall between two French doors in a period house highlights a fine piece of furniture but also draws attention to the fact that it is off-center. Placing it in the middle of the wall creates a sense of harmony between the doors and the armoire—and in the arrangement as a whole.

LEFT Different functions within this open-plan living area progress logically from cooking to dining to relaxing. The contrast between a contemporary modular sofa and an antique table reinforces a sense of division.
ABOVE This understairs area is an appealing setting for a long, low bench. Felt pads, sheepskin rugs, and scatter cushions made with Moroccan fabrics add essential comfort.

SUGAR   FLOUR   TEA   PASTA   COFFEE

Cooking and eating

In many homes today, the kitchen area is a center where people meet to cook, eat, and relax, so what it looks like and how it contributes to the atmosphere of your home is as important as its efficiency. The main considerations when designing a kitchen area are whether to choose freestanding or built-in units and furniture, or a mixture, and whether the space will function purely as a kitchen or be used for other activities. Flooring, walls, work surfaces, and storage all provide the potential to combine ancient and modern, either in relation to the structure of the building—a modern stainless-steel kitchen in a period house, for example—or by mixing old and new elements like an antique hutch, salvaged faucets, a ceramic sink, and a contemporary counter.

THIS PAGE Industrial stainless-steel fixtures and appliances combine with Japanese-style elements, including a traditional storage cupboard, drawer units, shoji screens, paper lantern, and slate floor, to create a precise and orderly kitchen area. **OPPOSITE** Organized along a single wall, freestanding stainless-steel fixtures, a blue stone counter, and a professional-size stove are compatible with the raw industrial structure of a former brick factory. The pine country table and natural-colored rug add textural contrast.

Select and work with materials, colors, and finishes that are in keeping with the style of kitchen you want. Hard-edge materials such as concrete, metal, and glass are suitable for an industrial style, whereas natural ones like wood, stone, and slate are suited to a country-style kitchen. Use contemporary, salvaged, or ancient materials as appropriate or combine different materials to create a variety of styles and effects. For example, you could insert a piece of marble from an old dairy between sections of new wood, or lay old tiles and cover them with glass to provide a sealed work surface. Give all old surfaces a professional cleaning and reseal wood with tung oil to make it water-repellent and protect it against staining. However, it may be difficult to remove all stains—and smells—from old wood and stone.

Keep the design and overall concept simple, functional, and easy to clean and maintain. Practicality, safety, and ease of use are paramount in a kitchen area. The minimum requirement is a core of permanent work surfaces, cooking equipment, and storage units: A simple arrangement of appliances and built-in units with a durable countertop, possibly along one wall or in a central block to define and contain the kitchen area, provides all the essential basics.

Painting built-in units and shelving the same color as the walls and investing in a good-quality work surface, possibly made from recycled wood or slate, is cost-efficient and avoids the anonymity of mass-produced designs. It will also create a harmonious contrast to a feature element such as a Victorian plate rack or an old glass-and-metal display cabinet for storing glassware or herbs. Depending on your budget, you can elaborate on the basics, such as installing high-specification industrial equipment like stainless-steel shelving for storing pans and heavy cookware.

LEFT Within sight from the whole space, well-chosen elements and a freestanding stove provide a multifunctional, low-key kitchen area in a loft. The homemade high-level table is both a convenient work surface and an alternative place to sit and eat. A section of wall by the door, a useful device for containing storage shelves, and a change in flooring are reminders of the loft's original division of space. OPPOSITE The former living room of a nineteenth-century country house is now a general family area for cooking, eating, and relaxing, with a long pine table and colorful Arne Jacobsen chairs. Installing kitchen appliances and fixtures in parallel blocks behind a low wall means that the whole area works on all levels. Overspill storage in a separate pantry and a laundry area through the door on the left facilitate this low-key arrangement.

For appliances, it is generally best to choose modern products. Although traditional enamel stoves work well in an eclectic arrangement of elements, they are in high demand and short supply. Finding and possibly reconditioning a secondhand traditional refrigerator can take many weeks. Instead, check out appliances for commercial kitchens, such as oversize designs in heavy-duty materials like steel and reinforced glass. An alternative is to buy standard appliances and combine function and aesthetics by concealing them with fascia panels or by housing them creatively — for example, slot a stove into a line of freestanding, low-level, country-style cabinet and drawer units, and cover the units with a stainless-steel, marble, or slate counter. (Line any wood surfaces adjacent to the sides of the stove with metal plates to prevent the risk of fire.) Or install a refrigerator in an antique armoire. (Remove the cabinet base for stability, and make sure the doors of the armoire and refrigerator align. If they don't, remove the lower section of the door frame for access.) Alternatively, slot the fridge into a custom-built box with an optional door. The box can be made from salvaged tongue-and-grooving or sheets of copper or steel on a plywood frame.

If your kitchen is also an eating area, choose a table and chairs for their aesthetic appeal and the color, shape, and texture they add to an ancient and modern environment, as well as for their efficiency. In a contemporary all-white kitchen area, for example, an antique table with aluminum chairs is an inviting place to sit; or combine a rosewood table with translucent plastic chairs. Keep to a core group of textures and materials to create a harmonious arrangement, and introduce single blocks of enlivening colors and textures, such as a modern table with a colorful laminated surface in contrast to old floorboards.

Whether a dining table and chairs are part of a kitchen, a general living are elements that work within the overall environment and al

The modest structure of this wooden beach house, built in the 1920s, sets a standard of practical simplicity for decoration and furniture. Painted walls and floors in bright new colors update the structure of the space, and the scrubbed bare-top painted table and thrift-shop country chairs combine to create an easy-to-maintain kitchen and dining area.

The imposing structure of this sixteenth-century farmhouse, with stone floors, bare plaster walls, and a walk-in fireplace, requires furniture of a similar scale to balance the proportions and architectural style of the room. The circular table, made from a piece of plywood set on wooden blocks, was cut to fit the space.

in a separate room, aim to create a welcoming combination of
Jaxed and pleasurable dining.

In this open-plan New York loft with painted walls and polished floorboards throughout, the challenge was to create a focus for different activities without compromising a sense of integration. Parallel shelving with a display of collectable glass is a simple and effective way of defining the dining area, which has a home-made table and contemporary aluminum chairs.

This intimate dining alcove within a vast New York loft provides ample opportunity for juxtaposition between ancient and modern architecture and elements. The matte surfaces of an ancient wooden Indian table, plain chairs, and elegantly simple copper lamps contrast with the high-gloss painted paneling, black wooden floors, and a magnificent window.

THIS PAGE This linen-tented, wooden four-poster bed provides enclosure and privacy in contrast to the sense of space, light, and openness in a London loft. Linen curtains, a fake-fur throw, and a kilim counterbalance the hard-edged architecture.

OPPOSITE An artful arrangement of an antique armoire, bed frame, and floor-lamp base in a New York bedroom is given an inexpensive update with a simple injection of color. The pink mohair blanket adds warmth and vibrancy.

Sleeping

A good night's sleep is vital to our physical, mental, and emotional well-being. Creating the best possible environment for this within an ancient and modern space means balancing a high level of comfort, for example, from a good-quality mattress, with well-chosen furniture, textiles, lighting, and objects from the past. The combination can be as direct as a rustic nineteenth-century Indian bed in a pared-down room or a romantic antique Spanish chandelier in an otherwise modern interior. Too much visual stimulation or too many pieces of furniture can conflict with the area's main function, so limit the elements to essentials to promote rest and relaxation.

A+M

A bed can be an ornamental decorative feature or a simple base and mattress with color and texture provided by the bedlinen. A contemporary futon standing on rush-covered tatami mats and covered with an antique silk quilt can be as inviting and beautiful as an antique four-poster with crisp linens and plaid blankets. Consider a bed in the context of its surroundings, and give it space and definition regardless of its worth.

Period beds normally have substantial frames that isolate them from other elements in a space, making them the focal point. An antique French bed with ornate wooden carving, a simple Victorian single bed with an iron frame, or an eighteenth-century four-poster would be a distinctive centerpiece in any ancient and modern environment. For maximum contrast, install it in a contemporary space, or in a period home offset it against a wall with a single block of color, wooden paneling, or uneven plaster.

If a bed is to be part of an ensemble of ancient and modern pieces, try to balance it with another item. For example, a contemporary metal bed could be balanced by an Indian armoire. Also, position elements to create a sense of symmetry, such as by placing a pair of modern reading lamps on each side of an antique bed; add a large rug for contrast and definition.

Clutter-free is stress-free, so provide ample storage for clothing and belongings. A combination of hanging space and drawers or shelving can accommodate all the basics. This can be an inexpensive option like a row of traditional peg hooks with various sizes of baskets underneath for T-shirts, jeans, and socks, or a more costly one such as an extensive Shaker-style wall of built-in drawers and cupboards. Alternatively, install an architectural feature: conceal storage behind a low partition wall or a series of floor-to-ceiling sliding panels.

All the care and planning that goes into creating a welcoming and soothing sleeping area means it can become an overflow or alternative space for general relaxation. A bed can be an ideal setting for reading, a relaxing massage, listening to music, or, if you have children, playing. It is important to choose and position one so that it will accommodate all its uses and users. To vary light levels and alter the atmosphere, install a dimmer switch to a central ambient light, for example, a glass pendant or Japanese paper lantern. A gooseneck or other directional lamp on a bedside table or on the floor next to your bed is necessary for reading and can be turned upward as an uplight.

THIS PAGE, TOP TO BOTTOM
Positioning this simple bed base and mattress to line up below a prominent roof apex makes the bed central and important to the area and promotes a sense of order and symmetry.
In this pared-down historic country house, luxury bedside lighting combines with basic inexpensive elements and a colorful blanket to create a comfortable and welcoming bedroom.
The difference in scale between this contemporary, hospital-style bed and the high ceilings in a nineteenth-century house creates an enchanting Alice-in-Wonderland illusion. The contrast between the scale of the prints and the standard-size door compounds the effect.
A confident mix of raw brickwork, gentleman's-club-style paneling, and ancient Indian doors creates a bold and exotic environment for an oversize bed with silk bolster and dust ruffle.

In spite of the industrial plastic pleating installed to provide optional separation, the antique Indian bed and bedlinen create a romantic sleeping area. Positioning the bed away from the window optimizes the sense of connection in an open-plan space.

Antique bathtubs like this zinc one with a
fake wood surround—or even a
commonplace Victorian rolltop version
with ball-and-claw feet—look good, so it
is worth making them a central feature in
an ancient and modern space. Installing
a toilet and shower in separate
compartments in this Paris apartment
keeps the contrasts between elements
and architecture direct and simple.

Bathing

Showering or bathing is a daily necessity as well as an opportunity to soothe tension and revitalize your body. The success of a bathing area depends on a good supply of hot water, effective water pressure, ventilation, and heating. The efficiency of modern pumps and thermostats in providing this essential—and usually invisible—backup for appliances means that it is possible to experience a back-pummeling performance shower even with an antique showerhead.

The patina and shapes of bathtubs, basins, and other fixtures—ancient or modern—make strong visual statements within a space. A Victorian rolltop tub in front of a wall of glass bricks in a loft is an example. Alternatively, combine ancient and modern fixtures and details: an antique zinc bathtub with a contemporary glass basin and a mono-block faucet, or standard modern bathroom furniture offset with antique mirrors. This way, clinical efficiency can be balanced with aesthetics and worn textures.

Floor-to-ceiling and wall-to-wall tiling is an effective method of waterproofing, but painted plaster or wood can be given adequate protection by applying a glossy glaze. Combining tiling with another material is an opportunity to introduce contrasts. In a Japanese-style bathing area, slate tiles on the walls, floor, and around the bathtub are offset by paper-and-wood sliding shoji screens.

How a bathing area relates to the rest of a space, such as whether it interconnects with a sleeping area, requires consideration and planning. While some areas suggest a perfect setting for a bathtub or shower—under a sloping roof, in front of a grand fireplace, or in the bay window of a sleeping area—it is important to check with a plumber before you progress with any plans. Installing or moving water pipes and drains is expensive and disruptive, so the cost-efficient option is often to optimize what exists.

Consider how much privacy you need to feel comfortable. In a loft-style apartment in London, positioning an antique rolltop so it can be seen from every part of the open-plan environment gives the space a sense of freedom and integration. However, before you take down walls to create openness, consider the privacy factor from all angles—including from the outside looking in. If you are concerned about interruption by people you live with, a division of some kind is essential. Even if you live alone, bathing is sometimes more relaxing in an enclosure of some kind. Translucent sliding panels in plastic or glass, shoji screens, low-budget hospital screens (available from professional equipment suppliers), or inexpensive shower curtains all provide a degree of separation without blocking light.

Install suitable low-level or adjustable ambient lighting for relaxing in a bath, with task lighting beside a mirror. Bathroom lighting must conform to safety standards, so if you want to install antique lights, have them checked by a professional.

LEFT Shoji screens provide optional separation between sleeping and bathing areas. Another screen to the right separates this section from a living area. ABOVE The juxtaposition of an antique bathtub and an industrial brick wall is too good to hide. A sliding plywood panel can provide privacy when needed.

Working

Planning an area to work in means assessing how important the activity is to you and how much time you spend on it, then deciding on the equipment you need. This will determine the amount of space required. Running a business from home is not the same as sitting down to pay bills or process a weekly grocery list online. Each requires a very different setup and commitment of resources and space, and presents very different options for ancient and modern combinations.

If you work from home, it is worth committing a separate space as a work area, with specialized furniture and lighting, a phone, computer equipment, and other technology. The advantages are that it will provide privacy and quiet, and you won't disturb others while you work. You will also be able to consider its style and arrangement in its own right rather than in relation to another area—and if space is not at a premium, you will be less likely to underestimate your needs.

Finding the right desk for your computer—and the right chair to go with it—is essential. It can be difficult to find an antique desk with a worktop that is the right height and depth for using a keyboard, so

it may be preferable to use a custom-built computer desk or cart and offset it with ancient furniture and details such as a wooden or metal filing cabinet or an antique kilim to add texture, color, and individuality.

If you set up a work area as part of a dual-function space, try to make sure it receives adequate light and fresh air—or use mobile furniture for easy crossovers between different activities. Consider the position of a computer screen and avoid the glare of a backlit screen or reflections of light on a screen. If necessary, modulate incoming light with blinds.

Office furniture and equipment are not easy to camouflage, so avoid using part of a living area as a home office unless you plan to conceal it in some way. Divisions such as contemporary sliding panels or salvaged folding doors, possibly across a section of the relaxing area, will provide efficient screening.

Creating a small-scale work area for projects like household management or dealing with personal finances is a good idea since these activities do not logically integrate with any others. A desk with drawers or compartments is useful for filing documents. Choose and position it to integrate with the overall plan of the space.

ABOVE A mid-twentieth-century adjustable lamp makes an effective contrast with an elegant rosewood desk. Antique desks add character to home offices, but custom-made contemporary desks are preferable for long periods of computer work. BELOW LEFT Placing this Arts and Crafts desk and chair next to a window creates a light and appealing work area.

THIS PAGE This flip-down antique desk looks like a chest of drawers, but it contains a comprehensive system of compartments and drawers—ideal as a part-time worktable for dealing with household bills and correspondence.
OPPOSITE BELOW RIGHT Plastic screens attached to a wooden beam blur the impact of a professional office and provide important separation in a family space.

Loft conversion

ANCIENT ORIENTAL LIVING IN A CONTEMPORARY OPEN-PLAN SPACE

A loft-style apartment in London's South Bank area is a large open-plan space with flexible divisions between areas, along the lines of a traditional Japanese interior. It was originally three apartments, two with spectacular views and a third at the back of the building. The conversion, by the architectural firm Ushida Findlay, combines the positive aspects of all three spaces with a bold mix of natural materials in an imaginative adaptation of oriental living.

The apartment is now an inverted L-shape, the base of which is a wide space with a wall of windows and glass. This incorporates two of the three original apartments and has stunning views of Tate Modern, the River Thames, and the city skyline. Formal arrangements of a traditional

MAIN PICTURE The arrangement of the main living area takes full advantage of a magnificent view. Traditional Chinese furniture and a curving wall of bamboo add color, shape, and enlivening juxtapositions.
LEFT Since views are such a big feature of the space, many elements are oriented toward windows, like this chair and footstool, which are positioned for quiet contemplation.

long, low table, sofa, armchairs, and a high-back chair and footstool orient this area toward the view. Antique Chinese cabinets provide storage for entertainment equipment and books.

A curving bamboo wall sweeping down the length of the apartment connects the front and back areas—incorporating the third original apartment—and emphasizes their different functions. The front of the space is a social public area, while the back is private. The bamboo wall also conceals storage for housewares, clothes, and books.

The main entrance to the apartment is a bamboo-covered door midway along the bamboo wall. Opposite this is a wide opening made from stained wooden beams, which looks like an oriental football goal, with a wooden crossbeam extending on each side to connect with and form part of a kitchen on the left and a tatami room on the right.

In Japan space is measured by the number of tatami mats—mats made from straw and covered in rushes—that fit into it. The dimensions of the tatami room are based on this precise method of measurement. The basic structural element in the space, a wooden base and frame that slot together without nails, was made in Japan, then dismantled and shipped to the site. Traditional shoji screens—wooden frames with paper infills—slide in the frame to conceal or reveal the area within. Tatami mats provide a soft, textural base for low-level living, and there is an antique low table for traditional

Japanese dining. The area is also used for relaxing and as an alternative sleeping space; futons are stored in a built-in closet in the room.

The appreciation of natural materials and the Japanese influence throughout the loft extend to uneven slate floor tiles, an authentic textured render on the walls in the main living area, and textured Japanese wallpaper in the tatami room. This influence is also evident in the use of lanterns to draw attention to different areas in the space.

The kitchen area next to the tatami room is less purist, although no less ingenious. Traditional redwood cabinets contain standard kitchen equipment, and the room incorporates an authentic cabinet for storage. Shoji screens divide the kitchen from the rest of the space, or slide open to offer views into the tatami room.

The bamboo corridor starts as a wide opening alongside the sitting area, narrows as it passes the kitchen and the tatami room, and continues toward the main sleeping and bathing areas at the back of the apartment. This is the private part of the space; a shoji screen across the opening allows it to be closed off from the rest of the apartment.

Whereas the bamboo wall is simply inspired by oriental style, the tatami room and shoji screens are imaginative installations of traditional Japanese design elements. They work well in the scale of the space and are a brilliant solution for dividing the loft into different areas without blocking light or compromising a sense of openness and connection.

BELOW The curving lines of the chair and the comfort of the antique footstool, positioned near a textured plaster wall, create a welcoming individual seating area.
RIGHT The bamboo wall runs the entire length of the apartment, connecting every area within the space. It also provides extensive hidden storage.

Interior architecture

CONTEMPORARY MINIMALISM IN A NINETEENTH-CENTURY NEW YORK TOWNHOUSE

An ornate marble fireplace is a striking original feature in the main living area of this pared-down space and influences the formal arrangement of furniture. The shapes of a low table— a slice of a tree trunk with bark on both sides yet planed to a smooth finish on top—and flowering plants add organic forms without deviating from a powerful orderly scheme.

In this apartment in a Manhattan townhouse, nothing is left of the nineteenth-century configuration of space or architectural detailing, apart from a marble fireplace and sash windows at the front of the building. As architect Stephen Roberts demonstrates with this precision-engineering style of architecture, it is possible to combine an ancient building with rigorous minimalist reduction without sacrificing a perfect finish.

The apartment has its own entrance and extends the full length and width of the original townhouse, from the sash windows in the front to a courtyard garden at the back, which is entered through modern metal-frame French doors. Although the interior has been reinvented to create a purist contemporary environment, the space progresses in a conventional line from a formal sitting area to a kitchen area, a dining area, and finally to sleeping and bathing areas. The simple logic of this progression strengthens the scheme. It removes any conflict between the original design and layout of the space and how it works today, and focuses energy and attention on the overall sense of space, light, shape, and color.

Starting with the hall and the view ahead into the work area—a tall, slim slot of space that runs half the length of the apartment behind the sitting and dining areas and has a built-in worktable—it is apparent that this project is about taking control and not deviating from a plan because of an original lack of precision, misalignment, or architectural detail.

Every area is at once spartan and impressive in its simplicity, finish, and sense of order and space. Yet there is no lack of shape or texture. The more you look, the more you see. The main living area is an ideal example. Two identical off-white Paolo Lenti sofas in felt upholstery face each other across a low table made from a section of a tree trunk; the bark on the sides contrasts with the smoothness of the wood. A Charlotte Perriand bookcase from around 1920, without books, and white low-level cabinets with lacquered metal doors suspended along one wall add shape and practical storage. The cabinets hold objects like candlesticks and bowls that are not always in use. Apart from colorful Plexiglas rods, which stand above the fireplace or on the floor by the window to reflect light, the area is without color or decoration.

A floor-to-ceiling opening connects with the rest of the space and leads past a slim kitchen to the dining area. The kitchen consists of two identical low-level blocks of units, parallel to each other like the sofas, with built-in appliances and stainless-steel countertops. Everything is put away. To make a cup of tea, it is necessary to take out a pan, tea bag, and cup. Brilliant storage and planning make this a simple undertaking.

The dining area is the plainest in the apartment, with a horizontal light above a classic Knoll table and chairs. Benches provide alternative seating. Any pieces of furniture that are not in use are kept in the work area, which is accessible through a doorway in the wall behind the table. Beyond the dining area is a raw-wood bed designed by the owners.

The front and back windows are the main sources of daylight, apart from two narrow ones with sandblasted glass in the middle of one side of the apartment. Consequently, it was important to allow light to reach the center of the space. Folding glass-and-metal doors provide optional separation between the dining and sleeping areas. The glass is opaque to provide privacy without blocking light. With light behind them, the doors glow a pale green. Wraparound white ceilings, walls, and poured terrazzo floors add to the clean, pure aesthetic of the space and to the sense of light.

Furniture and objects, including a Georges Jouve vase from the 1950s, are kept to a minimum. This is typical of the pure aesthetic of the apartment. Simply reducing it to a series of finely planned areas with extensive storage liberates the space from excessive furniture and detail so that a simple bed or a table with benches fulfills all requirements. It is a triumph of the overall scheme that such diverse elements as a heritage fireplace from the nineteenth century and a contemporary raw-wood table work so well together.

BELOW Although the apartment is open-plan, each area is contained and partly separated by the architecture without any loss of integration. This arrangement is supported by furniture that focuses on one activity, such as a vintage Knoll table and chairs in the dining area.
RIGHT A narrow kitchen, which slots in between the sitting and dining areas, consists of two parallel blocks of cabinets with stainless-steel counters. One counter is a seamless plane; the other contains a stovetop and two sinks. The kettle is from a New York flea market.

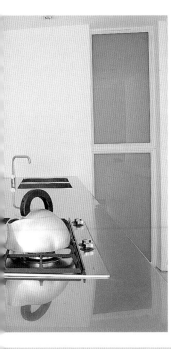

ABOVE The apartment extends the full length of a basement area. This view, from the bedroom at the back, looks toward the sitting area at the front of the house. Glass doors provide optional separation without blocking light from the central core of the space.

LEFT Display is selective within this minimal white space, yet it introduces vital contrasting color, shape, and form. In the sitting area, a sculpture by Vasa sits on the floor by an original window or on the mantel. Ceramics by Georges Jouve in the kitchen and dining areas complete the art list. The insides of the shutters are plain—without moldings—in keeping with the minimal interior. The box beneath the window conceals a cast-iron radiator.

ELEMENTS

"Have nothing in your house that you do not know to be useful and believe to be beautiful." William Morris

THIS PAGE An inherited hutch is the centerpiece of this eclectic mix of furniture, textiles, and artifacts, which includes Liberty chairs, a modern oval table, and a graphic banner made from an African kuba cloth. PREVIOUS PAGES The worn surfaces of a painted wooden chest of drawers and a plaster wall connect and reduce the impact of their intense colors. The random brushwork on the wall offsets the fine markings on a contemporary ceramic by Rupert Spira.

Whether you are putting together a capsule collection of essential furniture, reviewing what you already have, or looking for a specific piece, the way the elements are combined is central to the success of an ancient and modern space.

There are many variations on how old and new items of furniture can be used in an interior. Juxtapose modern pieces with an ancient architectural feature or add antique furniture to a modern space. Group old and new items to create contrast—contemporary aluminum chairs with an old oak dining table, for example—or use the texture and color of an upholstery fabric to link a sofa with armchairs from a different period.

If you are mixing ancient and modern items from diverse cultures or styles, stick to predominantly simple shapes and pieces that are made from one material such as wood or metal, or upholstered in one fabric. An example is a collection of antique wooden chairs contrasted with a contemporary metal table, or an eclectic mix of an old country wooden chair, a contemporary plastic chair, and a contemporary metal chair with an antique country table. It is easier to combine elements that are not combinations in themselves. To this simple and well-defined mix it is then possible to add a decorative item without undermining an overall sense of harmony. For example, a decorative metal-and-glass low table could be combined with a group of secondhand armchairs re-covered in gray linen.

If you inherited your furniture or if it has accumulated over the years, fitting it into an ancient and modern space may present a challenge. Deciding which pieces to keep, which can be modified, and which may need to be removed comes down to personal preference. Looking beyond the furniture to the structure of a space, such as the color of the walls or flooring, can suggest how to create an ancient and modern environment using existing pieces. If you love a particular item or it is important to you as a family heirloom, make it a centerpiece or a starting point when you review the possibilities.

This chapter explores a wide range of options for using sofas, tables, chairs, and storage furniture to enrich an ancient and modern space while fulfilling the practical needs of a contemporary home.

Furniture for relaxing

Furniture that encourages relaxation is an essential element in a living space, whether you prefer a traditional cushioned sofa upholstered in suede or antique kilims, a French nineteenth-century wrought-iron daybed with a muslin mattress, or a mid-twentieth-century iconic armchair. Depending on the arrangement you want—an informal group of antique armchairs and a linear modern sofa, for example, or an eclectic mix of nineteenth-century armchairs in a modern apartment—ancient furniture offers great potential for enlivening combinations. Reupholstering a sofa or armchair or making a slipcover for it, provides an opportunity to totally reinvent it. A Victorian chesterfield that looks pretty and unremarkable in chintz becomes a very different piece of furniture if it is upholstered in gray mohair. Or leave worn, even threadbare, antique upholstery like damask or tapestry in its original state for contrast and a sense of history in a contemporary environment.

A mix of antique fabrics and the patina of antique frames will connect very different styles and periods of furniture, whether the frames are wood, wicker, bamboo, or cast iron. For example, in a New York loft, a baroque dark wood bench-style sofa with a velvet seat cushion, a Victorian parlor sofa in flock velvet, and faux bamboo armchairs with silk seat covers coexist in artful harmony.

The colors and textures of antique fabrics work well with modern structural treatments like bare floorboards or plain brick, stone, or plaster walls. Or, for a harmonious combination of ancient furniture with a contemporary space, re-cover the pieces in an unobtrusive fabric like ticking or felt. Reupholstering individual pieces in the same color but different fabrics—cream wool, linen, and cotton, for example—or in the same fabric in a family of colors—linen in shades of yellow and ocher—will unify even eccentric items.

Antique sofas and chairs may require rebuilding or padding before they are reupholstered. This is expensive and can change a pleasingly misshapen piece into a plain one. If you buy furniture from a dealer, ask for advice on this, and if you plan to repair an original fabric, check with an upholsterer. Slipcovers are a good way to unify or simplify elements without detracting from their original state.

Contemporary sofas and chairs, with their lightweight frames, linear designs, and high-specification stretchy, stain-resistant, or blended fabrics in a good range of colors add comfort and pace to an ancient and modern interior. In a converted English cowshed with stone walls and flagstone floors, an electric-blue foam-based sofa with a metal frame provides a single seating option. It is as practical as it is dynamic—in summer children sit on it with wet swimsuits. Modular seating is flexible—it can be split into individual seats or put together along a wall in an industrial loft conversion or into the corner of a cottage.

The effect a contemporary piece has on an interior can be very different from that of an ancient one. For example, the simplicity of line and construction of a Terence Woodgate sofa draws attention to the objects around it. This is not a caution against contemporary design, but an affirmation of it. Any piece that sparks a review of the other elements in a space is a positive addition since it can result in a more pared-down, harmonious interior. If introducing a contemporary design makes other furniture look out of place, edit your existing pieces, ancient and modern, and review the overall space. Adding a rug or changing a wall color, for example, can provide a vital link between ancient and modern elements.

THIS PAGE The way the velvet has softened and faded on this old chesterfield is part of the sofa's appeal. Pragmatic mismatching repairs add to its idiosyncratic form.

OPPOSITE, TOP TO BOTTOM
The classic club aesthetic in this New York loft includes shining wood floors, chrome adjustable lamps, zebra skins, and traditional worn leather armchairs. The Antony chair by Jean Prouvé, like many iconic mid-twentieth-century chairs in demand for contemporary homes, was originally designed for commercial use.

Different shades and textures of white connect an expansive tweedy sofa (originally designed by Florence Knoll in 1954), a contemporary paper lantern, and nineteenth-century wooden paneling in this Paris apartment.

The shape of this modern Swedish chair in metal, wood, and leather provides comfort in an open-plan area without blocking light and views across the space or access to the outdoors.

THIS PAGE Using black vinyl to re-cover the seat pads on a set of ordinary plywood café chairs updates and upgrades them.
OPPOSITE LEFT A Knoll table and a set of classic Knoll chairs with woven leather seats and backs add warmth and texture to a pared-down contemporary setting.
OPPOSITE CENTER The curving backs of these Eames chairs contrast with the strong lines of nineteenth-century paneling, recycled floorboards, and a contemporary table.
OPPOSITE RIGHT The worn texture and irregular shape of these benches, found in the street, contrast with the straight lines and hard surfaces of an Art Deco apartment.

Practical chairs and tables

Hardbacked chairs, benches, and tables are versatile items. They are mainly used for dining areas, but can be utilized throughout a space. For example, a circular pine Victorian table and a contemporary bentwood chair placed by a window make a welcoming reading area. A contemporary glass-top and metal-frame table is useful for storage and display in a bedroom, an old wooden refectory bench is ideal for a hall, and a wooden chair of any period provides a warm dressing chair in a bathroom.

Unlike soft furniture, these practical items are difficult to modify. Whereas it is possible to diminish the grandeur of an eighteenth-century baroque armchair or elevate a Victorian parlor sofa with upholstery, a hardbacked dining or occasional chair is what it is. A neoclassical walnut one is redolent of bygone wealth and status. A rustic or ethnic chair, simply constructed from natural materials, retains a sense of the resourcefulness of the time when it was made. Painting it simply changes its color.

However, the context in which these practical items are used changes the way they are perceived. In a pared-down modern environment, the simplest ancient dark-wood chair will take on a powerful silhouette, while the elegant simplicity of a bentwood, Shaker ladderback, or African ironwood chair will add contrast and character to an area of soft seating as well as provide an alternative place to sit. In Gert van de Keuken's Art Deco apartment in Paris, pieces of furniture found in the street—an old wooden workbench and a pair of elongated low benches—are the focus of the dining area.

In addition to old chairs intended for use in the home, there are many practical and inexpensive alternatives designed for churches, schools, and community centers that transfer easily into an ancient and modern environment. The workaday integrity of these items makes them ideal for functional spaces such as eat-in kitchens and family bathrooms. Some of these chairs do not always align comfortably with dining tables, so check the height of the seats before you buy eight of them for your dining area. Bentwood or bamboo chairs with open backs are useful if space is at a premium because light will pass through them and they do not block views across an interior.

Chairs with high seats come into their own in a kitchen, next to a worktable or counter. Office or dressmaker's chairs and stools with a swivel base and adjustable heights are infinitely useful, sculptural designs.

If a table is to be used for dining, it is important to choose one—ancient or modern—that is the right size and shape for the space and that either complements or contrasts with the other elements. In a pared-down environment a dining table offers an opportunity to make a bold ancient and modern statement. For example, in a period house with plain walls and stripped floors, a primitive worm-eaten oak country table could be juxtaposed with a contemporary chandelier and aluminum chairs.

If you live in a compact space but like to invite friends for supper, an extendable table is a flexible solution. Options include an antique rosewood circular table with flip-up sides—one side can be kept up for regular use, and the dining area can be enlarged when required.

It is also possible to adapt a table intended for a particular purpose to another, quite different, use. For example, a former school worktable can be converted into a dining table by cutting down the legs and re-covering the top with a thin flexible sheet of copper, which can be lightly hammered or tacked to fit around the edges.

In a pared-down eighteenth-century living room, this wooden country table and chairs—bought at a flea market—provide an alternative seating area to a kitchen-dining space in the basement. A simple black plastic cover on the table contrasts with the white walls and ceiling and reflects light from a Georgian sash window. The patina on the chairs and table legs connects with the original wooden floor.

This light and spacious New York loft is a harmonious mix of flea-market finds, elegant handmade furniture such as this simple dining/work table, and a few contemporary pieces to update the overall look. Although they were made decades apart, these chairs are remarkably similar in design.

within a contemporary environment is more effective than a jumble or scattering of pieces. elements and the structure of the space bold and obvious.

Handmade in 1937 for a nearby village hall, this monumental table occupies one part of a vast studio in a former church. The wavy lines of the thick tabletop and the simple flowing outline and lightness of the Arne Jacobsen chairs make a dynamic ancient and modern combination.

In a pared-down cooking and eating area with white-painted walls, bare stripped floorboards, and clinical-style stainless-steel wall units, a Victorian jeweler's table looks like a contemporary sculpture. Used in isolation this way, a carefully chosen item of antique furniture acquires definition and a powerful presence.

Occasional tables and stools

Combining practicality and aesthetic appeal and working in support of larger items of furniture, occasional and low-level tables and stools help to create comfort and individuality in an ancient and modern space.

Occasional tables in sitting areas provide surfaces for books, lamps, and artifacts, and somewhere to sit and read a paper or eat lunch. In an ancient environment, contemporary glass-top or metal tables add a pool of reflection and light and produce a bold juxtaposition. If you are using two different tables in the same area, perhaps a low one for books and magazines and a console table for art displays, mix shapes and textures and even periods of design for variety and contrast. In furnituremaker Andrew Mortada's conversion of an artisan's studio in London, an Arts and Crafts console table with a display of African pots, baskets, and carvings is juxtaposed with a contemporary oval table with cast-concrete legs and a stone-effect top. The pared-down brick, glass, and concrete of the surroundings underline and unite the very different shape and construction of each table.

Low-level tables are primarily for storing books and magazines and displaying decorative items like an ethnic bowl for fruit. If you have a collection of remote controls for entertainment equipment, keeping them together on a low table in a contemporary glass dish or an African basket combines practical organization with an appealing decorative object. If you want to enliven a space with accent lighting on low-level tables, use contemporary glass or plastic globes to conceal bare bulbs.

Low-level stools provide indispensable supplementary seating and are useful surfaces on which to put a plate of food, a drink, a book, or your feet. From ancient African milking stools to Philippe Starck's colorful plastic Bubu or Prince Aha stools, these items enliven and add flexibility to an ancient and modern interior.

CLOCKWISE FROM TOP LEFT
A stool with woven string or raffia across a wooden frame is a common thrift-shop find. Use it as a low table or stool, and store it under a larger table or seat when not in use.
Designed for milking goats, this low African stool is a challenging place to sit, especially for long periods. However, it is an appealing sculptural piece for a contemporary space.
The fine construction and finish of this low table or stool is typical of traditional oriental crafts. Pieces like these are inexpensive and make ideal footstools for use with a sofa or hardbacked chair.
The natural texture of raffia suggests waterside living, so this cotton-spool stool is perfect in a Long Island beach house. Juxtaposed with a contemporary lamp and art, an ordinary table is transformed into the focus of a simple bedroom.
This long bench is used for displaying new work in ceramicist Rupert Spira's studio. The dark, worn ancient wood makes a bold contrast with pickled floorboards.
This mid-twentieth-century two-tier table is practical as well as decorative. Magazines and remote controls can be stored out of sight, leaving the top as a plain shape or a surface for display.

LEFT The simplicity of a blue-painted brick wall in an artist's New York loft pulls together an eclectic mix of pieces of furniture, including an old commercial chest of drawers. **ABOVE** This American country cupboard, with a repaired door, provides storage in a contemporary open-plan bathing area.

Storage

Storage is a key factor in creating an ancient and modern environment that is enjoyable and comfortable to live in. With adequate storage, which can be either built-in or freestanding or a mixture of both, the architectural elements become clearly visible, without the distraction of everyday clutter. Freestanding pieces like cabinets, chests, and armoires are features in their own right and can be used to create exciting contrasts with walls and floors.

Finding a balance between what to reveal or conceal and deciding on the kind of storage you want depends on the amount of space you need. Clothes, housewares, and appliances can be hidden in built-in storage that looks like a structural feature—a curving sculptural wall, for example, with access from either side, or a series of sliding panels that conceal a section of storage space. Architectural solutions like these, which contrast, or fuse, with the original structure work well with different styles of architecture.

Period storage pieces in bold shapes and colors can be especially effective in an ancient and modern environment: an ornate French armoire for china and glass in a kitchen area, for example, or a red lacquer oriental chest for storing bedlinen in a modern bedroom. If you want to use such a feature, it is worth providing built-in storage as a backup—over-filling a rustic hutch with china and glassware or piling books and magazines on an eighteenth-century chest of drawers will diminish the impact of the piece.

Country-style furniture, thrift-shop finds, and antiques can provide imaginative storage options. Examples include a food locker with a wooden frame and punched tin panels and shelves for a television cabinet; an old baker's trolley with slatted wooden shelves bleached from years of use for books or clothing; and an antique wooden chest of drawers as a feature piece in a contemporary bathroom for towels.

Look for hidden potential in old items. Repainting or stripping can transform an old chest, while changing the handles on an armoire will give it an instant new look. Pieces like these have great potential in an eclectic environment. They can be combined with other elements in a space, or a single piece can be the focal point in an interior, creating a bold juxtaposition with the architecture or other furniture.

In addition to providing infinite options for all kinds of storage, ethnic furniture has a powerful resonance in an ancient and modern interior. A nineteenth-century teak temple cabinet from Rajasthan for storing china, or a contemporary willow basket from Japan for vegetables or clothing adds a primitive simplicity to a modern interior. The key to relocating these items successfully to an ancient and modern environment is to use them for everyday storage.

Office or industrial equipment such as metal filing cabinets, safes, lockers, and cabinets can provide useful shelving, hanging, and drawer space and brings a contemporary focus to an ancient and modern interior.

The furniture throughout is a mix of individual pieces in traditional, iconic, and eccentric designs.

ABOVE Upstairs, folding
plastic dividers provide
optional separation within
an open-plan working,
relaxing, and sleeping area.
New skylights and a glass
panel that replaces a solid
gable end make this a light
and welcoming space. The
furniture includes a white
La Chaise chair designed by
Charles and Ray Eames and
a bed from India.
OPPOSITE The bold
architectural alterations—
emptying an Edwardian
house of all typical
references and introducing a
new open-plan configuration
—reinvent a conventional
home as an individual and
inspiring space.

The ground floor is effectively one room that
extends from the front to the back of the house with
dogleg stairs leading to the upper level. Walls and
ceilings are bare pink plaster, and the floor is
bleached oak. The big windows, including a bay
window at the front of the house, and external doors
are the only original Edwardian features. On one
side of the room, two nineteenth-century Gothic
stone fireplaces with antique mirrors hung above
them set the standard for an original, eclectic ancient
and modern style.

Powerful combinations of elements—a sculptural
modern chaise longue by Charles and Ray Eames
with an antique wooden bed from Rajasthan, an
antique Italian chandelier that once hung in a church
with a modern artwork, a nineteenth-century
jeweler's worktable with contemporary stainless-
steel restaurant cupboards—add a vital layer of
individuality, shape, and color. Similar confident
juxtapositions and connections of ancient and
modern architectural details, furniture, and objects
enliven the whole space.

The furniture throughout is a mix of individual
pieces in traditional, eccentric, and iconic designs. In
the sitting area, a traditional comfortable English
sofa covered in brown suede, a Jacobean-style
armchair with yellow silk upholstery, a Toshiyuki Kita
"wink" chair, and a decorative Victorian settee form
an appealing collection.

At the back of the ground floor, a step leads down
to a generous cooking and eating area. Along one
wall the entire kitchen slots into an immaculate low-
level white block with a refrigerator and dishwasher
in cabinets, a kitchen sink with laboratory faucets, a
work surface, and an electric stovetop. Below the
work surface, open stainless-steel racks—ideal for
saucepans, stacks of white plates, and African
wooden bowls—provide most of the storage space.
Foodstuffs are concealed in stainless-steel restaurant
cupboards on the opposite wall. The simplicity of
using either white or stainless steel projects a sense
of order and minimizes the kitchen's visual impact on
the overall space. It also offsets the texture and
shape of the nineteenth-century jeweler's worktable
and the sewing chairs in the dining area. Shaped like
a giant piece from a jigsaw puzzle and set against a
plain background, the sculptural outline of the table
becomes a key feature.

The upper level is for working, sleeping, and
relaxing. Part of the ceiling has been raised and glass
has been set into the gable end to create a
distinctive architectural feature and increase the
amount of light in the space. An antique Indian bed
in one corner can be screened with pleated white
plastic dividers designed for commercial use. On the
landing an identical screen provides optional
separation for the combined bathroom, dressing
room, and laundry area. The remaining roof space is
an additional compact sleeping area, with ladder
rungs for access and a new skylight.

In addition to space and openness, light and
reflection are keynotes in this building. Light from
the new skylights and the glass in the gable end add
a luminosity that filters through the stairs to the
ground floor. Mirrors and glass are positioned to
reflect light. Luxurious white velvet curtains on each
side of the window, a glitter painting on the wall, and
silk, velvet, and suede upholstery all contribute
shimmering or shining surfaces and finishes.

DETAILS

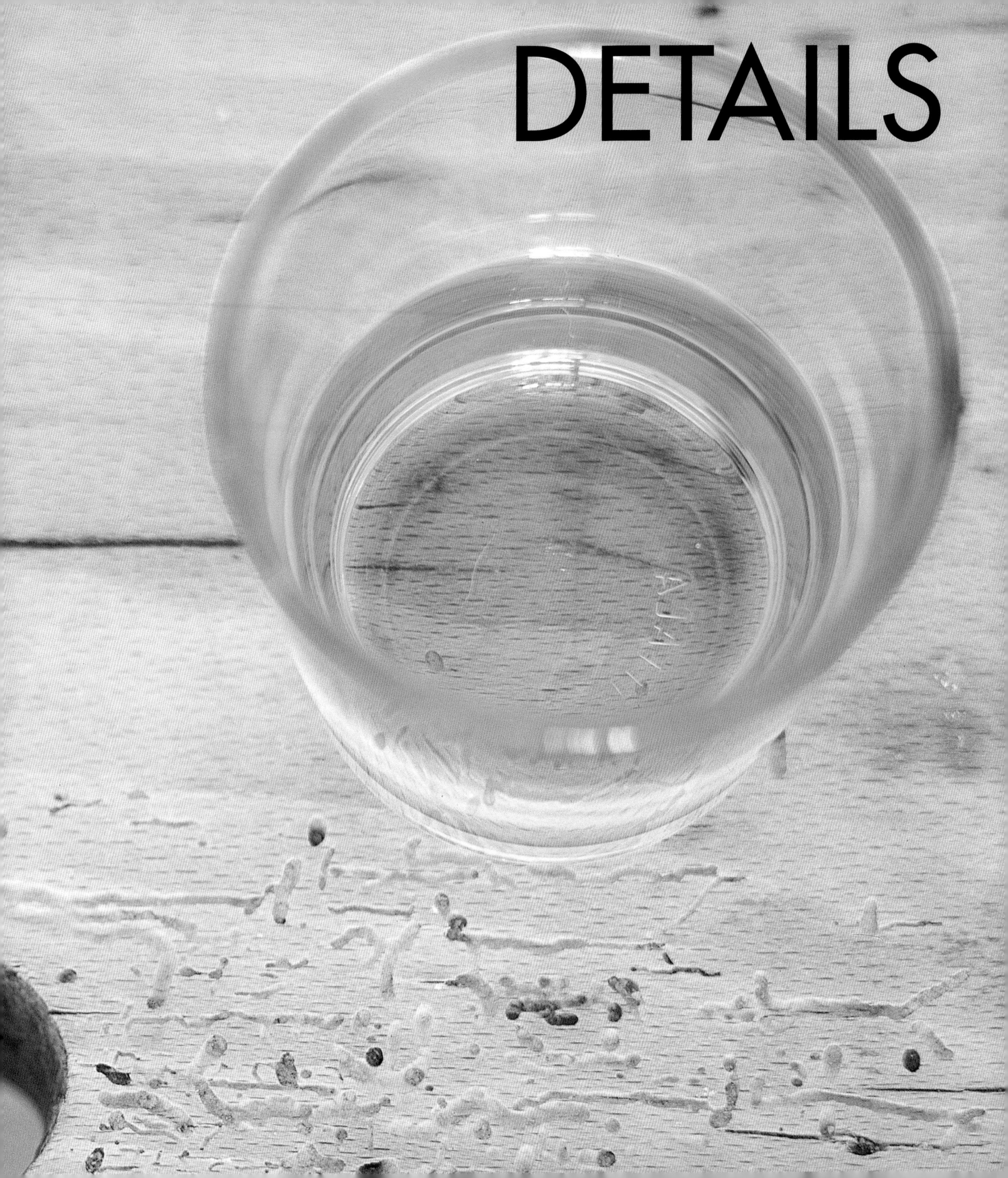

"God is in the details."

Mies van der Rohe

THIS PAGE An inspirational collection of flea-market finds, personal treasures, and a few well-chosen objects is displayed on a row of identical side tables in Gert van de Keuken's Paris apartment.
PREVIOUS PAGES The split and worm-eaten surface of a worker's bench, found in the street and now used as a table, presents a contrasting and textural backdrop to contemporary tableware.

Details add an essential layer of color, texture, and shape to a home. Decorative and functional objects, pictures, mirrors, textiles, lights, and fixtures all play a crucial part in defining an individual ancient and modern style.

Details can be used both in isolation and in combination with other features in a space. Making a single detail the focal point of an interior—for example, a contemporary chandelier made from concrete reinforcing bars and glass beads in a nineteenth-century townhouse, or an African goat's-milk bowl on a hand-hewn wooden pillar in an Art Deco apartment—creates an effective ancient and modern contrast between a detail and the architectural style of a space. Vibrant antique silk floor cushions on a concrete floor add visual punctuation to a contemporary interior; positioning a twentieth-century ceramic bowl on the mantel of a Georgian fireplace will bring the special qualities of both into focus.

Juxtapositions between details—used as single features or in compatible groups—and the furniture within a space can be similarly effective and direct. Examples include ancient and modern ethnic textiles, bowls, and artifacts with traditional and antique English furniture in a modern loft-style apartment, and antique French decorative mirrors, glass, and silk cushions with contemporary sofas, chairs, and tables in a pared-down interior.

Establishing connections between details and the structure of a space or the elements within it creates a very different ancient and modern environment. The collection of details can often include greater diversity, but the overall effect is less contrasting. In fashion designer Han Feng's New York loft, most of the details and furniture in a former light-industrial space are oriental, which gives the interior a sense of harmony and connection. Yet within various groups of furniture and details, there are bright yellow and red silk lanterns, purple and orange silk cushions, decorative wrought-iron birdcages, rustic bamboo stools and tables, twig baskets, and delicate lacquered cupboards and boxes.

This chapter shows how details of every kind, from paintings to teapots, can be used to create ancient and modern combinations that will personalize and enrich a home.

Display

Objects, artifacts, and pictures offer great potential for creating ancient and modern combinations, and the way they are displayed is an important consideration. Whether it is a collection of glass, ceramics, sculptures, paintings, or photographs; an artful cross-section of everything; or a single object, a display works well if it has shape, color, and a theme or an idea. It is therefore essential to maintain a sense of discipline both about the items you choose and the way you display them.

If you are combining several different objects, finding out which pieces work well together is a matter of trial and error. When assembling a line of ceramics for display, ceramicist Rupert Spira puts several pots together spontaneously, then reviews and edits them in order to achieve the best effect. Style forecaster Gert van de Keuken rarely moves an object once he has put it in his apartment, preferring to trust his instincts about what is right. Yet some people like to move objects around endlessly —sometimes displaying them on their own, sometimes grouping them with other artifacts—and discover and enjoy new compositions, juxtapositions, and connections every time.

THIS PAGE This powerful juxtaposition of 1970s columns of colorful laminated Plexiglas by Vasa and a restored 1860s marble fireplace is compounded by the minimal environment. OPPOSITE A bathroom window presents an unusual opportunity for a display. The sandblasted glass diffuses incoming light and masks the view, so attention is focused on the shapes and colors of the decorative glass bottles.

When selecting the object or objects to be displayed, it is important to consider the background and base as well as the scale, balance, and perspective of the display. For example, a large brown pot on a bamboo stool looks very different than the same pot on an oak chest of drawers. The way lighting affects the color, shape, and texture of different objects is another important factor.

Essentially, displaying an object or a collection of objects provides a means to contain it, which either isolates or connects it to the surroundings. Standing a contemporary plain dinner plate behind an antique Chinese lacquer box, or propping up a square of sandblasted glass behind an ancient object such as a tribal mask, can create an enlivening contrast of color and texture. Resting a piece of driftwood on a contemporary metal box or pinning a snapshot onto handmade paper provides textural contrasts and gives prominence to ordinary objects. The different styles of frames that contain pictures can either link the images to or contrast them with their surroundings. In a contemporary interior with white walls, displaying black-and-white archive prints in white mats and frames connects them with the structure of the space, whereas in a nineteenth-century home with gray paneled walls, colorful modern prints in wooden frames create a contrast. Both contemporary frames and simple old ones work well with modern images, although it can be difficult to find an antique frame that will fit a specific artwork.

Sculptures and other art objects can be contained by their background and setting, which could be a shelf above a fireplace, a deep window recess, or a cabinet. The surface on which a display stands is also important. A white shelf on a white wall is a dynamic architectural setting for eighteenth-century black-and-white prints. A restaurant cart with stainless-steel shelves provides a contrasting surface for a group of ancient ceramic bowls.

Objects
The vast range of objects that can be used in displays—anything from decorative items such as sculptures or bowls to utilitarian items like cooking utensils, or natural objects such as pebbles or fossils—provides great scope for ancient and modern combinations. Look for links between objects from different periods, and develop narratives by placing them together. A collection of wooden artifacts on a stainless-steel console table could include an ancient Japanese bowl, a mid-twentieth-century pot, and an Arts and Crafts box containing fragments of bones. A collection of ancient and modern glass candlesticks could be placed on a mantel. A display of identical objects—such as a string of contemporary papier-mâché lanterns along the center of an ancient farmhouse table—can have great impact.

RIGHT Displaying shells, wishbones, and small fragile items in a decorative antique glass protects them from damage and dispels a sense of clutter.
OPPOSITE Using a large glass vase to contain and display treasures like this animal skull and archive print is an effective way of combining disparate objects. The photographic print is by Simon Upton.

Natural objects like a sculptural branch, pebbles, or a collection of fossils can be as decorative as handmade ones. Interweave them with other objects in a display, or group small ones together. Create unusual combinations, such as shells in an antique ebony bowl or a piece of flint in a glass fishbowl.

The fact that old utensils like wooden spoons, chopping boards, wire strainers, and copper pots are designed to be used with ease and are made from natural materials explains why they are still used in contemporary kitchens. Along with china, flatware, and glass from antique and thrift shops, they already provide an ancient element in many modern households. To highlight the juxtaposition, store ancient pans, skillets, strainers, and casserole dishes on streamlined stainless-steel shelving and keep old wooden spoons in a stainless-steel measuring cup.

If you want to display china and glassware in your kitchen, consider any ancient and modern combinations in the overall context of the space. For example, if you have an antique hutch or painted cupboard, this is an ideal place to display contemporary china and glassware, or a mix of antique and contemporary tableware. A collection of old and new china, flatware, and glass will enable you to create ancient and modern table settings.

Old utility items work well in other areas of an ancient and modern space. Wooden boxes in a work area for storing desk equipment, baskets in a bedroom for organizing clothes, and storage jars in a bathroom for herbal remedies are examples.

This eclectic display of sparkly and reflective blue objects is an oasis of contrast and detail in a pared-down space with bare pink plaster walls and pickled-oak floors. The romance and decoration of the arrangement is balanced by the neutral surface of an ancient Indian table.

The temporariness of this spontaneous collection is part of its appeal. With a cupboard full of individual mismatched items, every meal and snack break has the potential to look different from the previous one. The shape of the chopping board used as a tray underlines the curves and roundness of the china cups and teapot.

The bold shape of this stainless-steel commercial cupboard provides high-specification kitchen storage and overrides any sense of clutter about the collection of Indian aluminum food pots on top. Distracting and discordant food packages are hidden behind sliding doors, making sure the kitchen area remains monochromatic.

d ephemeral as the combinations of flatware and china you choose when you set a table an arrangement of antique glass or ceramics.

The shape and texture of this Moroccan tea table provides an ancient ethnic juxtaposition to a spacious New York loft. The antique Moroccan teapot and traditional glasses are functional as well as decorative.

Every item of antique or secondhand glass on these shelves is animated by light from an adjacent window. In contrast to the delicate and reflective glass, a collection of found objects such as a bird's nest and pebbles seems well-defined and prominent. The strong lines of the architectural shelving contain the display.

Textiles

Textiles such as rugs, cushions, throws, blankets, curtains, and shades soften the hard lines and bare surfaces of structural features and furniture, and help make an ancient and modern environment warm and welcoming. Even simple ideas can have great impact: laying a contemporary gray felt rug on ancient floorboards to provide a soft base in a relaxing area, for example, or hanging a modern voile drape in front of an imposing stone-arch window to diffuse light and screen a view. An antique silk cushion on a contemporary modular sofa or a modern ethnic pillow on a worn velvet chesterfield adds visual and textural contrast as well as extra softness to firm pieces of furniture.

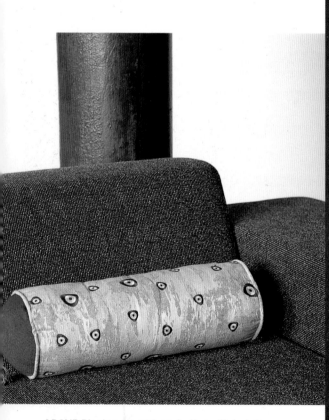

ABOVE Placing an antique Indian silk bolster on a contemporary tweed sofa brings out the color and weave of the fabrics and adds an additional layer of comfort.
RIGHT Used in Morocco for making hats, these large squares of red and blue-black felt have been sewn together with other squares to create a striking bedcover.

This African kuba cloth consists of complex graphic shapes sewn together. Shown off to good effect as a banner hanging from a mezzanine level in a studio, it provides separation between different areas.

Ornate wrought-iron curtain poles are an unusual decorative detail in this pared-down nineteenth-century converted church, yet are in perfect balance with the scale of the space.

ABOVE Curtains in this industrial conversion are a seasonal "hibernation" detail. Lengths of voile hung over steel tubing are easily removed in spring.
RIGHT This is the underside of a cowhide, painted with white paint. This way up, it is a simple graphic shape that adds a change of texture on a concrete floor and defines a seating area.
BELOW In this New York loft with concrete flooring and plain white walls, the seating area consists of big cushions covered in traditional Moroccan fabrics. The combination of pattern, color, and shape works well in this environment.

Natural textiles like wool, silk, cotton, and linen are good options for window treatments, cushions, and throws since they fade and soften with use.

Ancient textiles include old kilims, Persian rugs, animal hides, linen sheets, wool blankets, brocades, velvet cushions, ethnic fabrics, and hand-sewn and hand-printed silk, cotton, and linen. Select old textiles carefully to suit the use and location. A hard-wearing kilim runner or a Persian wool rug will stand up to everyday wear and tear in a living area. An antique quilt, on the other hand, is best used as a decorative daytime cover for a bed rather than as a practical alternative to a comforter or blanket.

Ancient and modern textiles can be combined in the same item. Examples include attaching a canvas panel to an antique linen sheet to make a curtain, combining antique silk with cotton to make bolsters, or using old linen on one side of a cushion and a contemporary hand-knitted square or piece of suede on the other side. If necessary, worn antique fabrics can be repaired by using contemporary unbleached canvas, leather, cotton lining, or ticking as a backing.

Natural textiles like wool, silk, cotton, and linen are good options for window treatments, cushions, and throws since they fade and soften with use. This adds a valuable layer of color and texture to a space, and their visual effect is similar to that of genuinely ancient fabrics. For the same reason, carpets and rugs in these materials make excellent floor coverings. Rush or coir matting is another good choice. In a factory conversion with bare brick walls and concrete floors, this natural material is compatible with the ambience and texture of the structural ones. Contemporary matting can also be used as a contrast to ancient elements in a space—on polished floorboards in a living area, for example.

Ancient ethnic textiles enliven contemporary interiors with color, contrast, pattern, and cultural references. Examples include a silk quilt or vibrant Moroccan fabric used as a throw on a minimalist modern sofa, or an Indian sari hung between the living and eating areas in an open-plan space. Antique kilims work well on bare floorboards in both modern and ancient environments and also make good pillow covers and throws. The fading colors of hand-dyed textiles like kilims and quilts combine brilliantly with the natural colors and textures of plain bare walls and floors, whether these are brick, stone, wood, or plaster.

Mirrors

Mirrors are practical and decorative and can add an extra architectural detail or change the view within an ancient and modern environment.

Practically, mirrors are vital features in bathing and dressing areas, and anywhere else where it is useful to see your reflection. They also help optimize the sense of light in a space.

Decoratively, they can be used to enliven a plain wall. For example, an antique French mirror could be leaned against a bare plaster wall. Or they can provide a focal point—a contemporary mirror cut to the same width as a Victorian fireplace, mounted in a plain frame and hung above the mantel, will draw attention to the combination of old and new elements. Antique mirrors in plain or ornate frames always look good and can be used in both ancient and modern environments in many different ways.

Architecturally, mirrors can extend an interior with views beyond the existing structure. Placing a mirror to reflect daylight from a window or skylight will instantly alter the perspective and quality of light in a space. Experiment with different positions to find the right

one. You can also position a mirror to reflect a key architectural feature. For example, a contemporary mirror could be placed to reflect a curving eighteenth-century staircase or exposed brickwork.

Using a simple sheet of mirror glass without a frame blurs the separation between it and the surface it is hanging on or leaning against. The mirror becomes a simple geometric shape that adds a dynamic detail and fits in with any style of architecture, ancient or modern. Examples are a rectangle of mirror glass in an eighteenth-century building, installed above an original mantelpiece and reflecting a window; or a circle of glass in a twentieth-century home, hung on a blue wall yet reflecting a yellow one. Mirrors like these present a perfect pool of reflection in contrast to the surface around them and can be cut to any shape or size. Antique mirrors that have been removed from their frames can be used the same way.

On a smaller scale, a mirror placed behind a favorite ceramic or wooden carving will enhance the presentation of the object with alternative views and reflected light. Mirror panels attached to the wall behind a display shelf will have a similar effect.

THIS PAGE An antique bathroom mirror with a plain frame sets the style of understatement and fine detailing in a New York loft. The sink and mirror configuration is one of a pair, set side by side along a wall of gray and white marble. OPPOSITE This ornate mirror is positioned above a fireplace in an open-plan living area to reflect ambient light. Framing the reflection of an industrial staircase is a bonus.

Pictures

A painting, a photograph, or a two-dimensional piece of artwork like a collage can provide a single key focal point in an ancient and modern space, or it can be used to define an area within an interior. An example of the latter is a series of plastic box-framed archive postcards placed alongside an antique dining table in a modern extension to an Arts and Crafts house.

Planning how and where to display a picture, whether it is a limited edition contemporary print, a family photograph, or a nineteenth-century oil painting, is about balancing it with its surroundings—ideally to the benefit of both. The three main points to consider are the content, color, and size of the work; the surface it will be displayed against; and the frame—all of which provide scope for ancient and modern juxtapositions or connections. For example, hanging an ancient, predominantly brown oil painting on a gray-painted wall in a contemporary space will add clarity and definition to the work.

The frame can be used either to connect a picture with its surroundings or to separate it from them. For example, a contemporary painting in muted colors could be framed in light wood to complement the image and make a visual connection with ancient wooden furniture. A modern black-and-white photograph combined with a plain white mat will add a dynamic contrast to an all-white contemporary interior.

Using identical frames and mats will unify different kinds of artwork, such as a collection of ancient and modern pencil sketches, oil paintings, and watercolors, without detracting from their content. Framing similar images in mismatching antique frames—such as a series of contemporary black-and-white family photographs in odd wooden frames—creates a lively display.

ABOVE The horizontal lines of a long ad-hoc table and exposed ceiling contain—and therefore frame—these abstract horizontal landscape paintings in English ceramicist Rupert Spira's farmhouse.
RIGHT Displayed without an ornate gilt frame, a traditional oil painting looks refreshingly strong, direct, and modern.

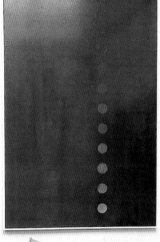

ABOVE The presentation, position, and scale of this photograph of a chair made by artists Langlands and Bell makes a dynamic exhibition feature in their London house. BELOW When hanging a picture, it is important to take into account the other elements in the room. The size and position of this antique table and contemporary painting balance each other.

Lighting

The right kind of lighting can transform the atmosphere in your home and introduce variation and contrast throughout a space. For example, it could be diffused in a dining or relaxing area and bright and direct in a work space. Planning and installing a comprehensive lighting system will reflect your individual style, contribute to the atmosphere of a space, and allow you to position or implement appropriate fixtures. For instance, including sockets in the floor will give you the flexibility to move lights around and is especially useful in large open-plan spaces.

Essentially, lighting falls into four categories. *Ambient* lighting is general background lighting that throws light over a wide area. *Task* lighting illuminates a specific activity. *Accent* lighting is used to highlight an architectural feature or painting. *Information* lighting maps out a space or illuminates a passageway or a change in floor level. It is therefore important to think about the kind of effects you want as well as the style of light fixtures. (It is always a good idea to review lighting whenever you carry out

MAIN PICTURE Scale is an important factor in finding an appropriate central light fixture. In this New York loft where everything is oversize, a flying-saucer lampshade looms over an interconnecting studio and living space. LEFT The classic shape and design of a bare light bulb, hooked onto a beam and hanging low over a kitchen table, is in keeping with a raw industrial space.

any structural alterations or decoration, as this presents an opportunity to extend or replace an existing system without additional disruption and expense.)

Antique fixtures, which are often decorative or grandiose, are ideal as ambient lighting and can become a focal point in a space. Central fixtures like antique chandeliers and glass pendants offer lots of potential for adding an enlivening detail to an ancient and modern interior. In Yvonne Sporre's unconventional London townhouse, for example, a teardrop church chandelier with the letter "M" (for Madonna) engraved on each crystal leaf makes a romantic central feature. In artists Langlands and Bell's modest home, traditional glass pendants provide a simpler central fixture in keeping with a minimal historic environment.

Antique table and floor lamps add shape, color, and variation to a space as well as satellite pools of light—either in conjunction with other, possibly contemporary, fixtures or as an independent option. In a New York loft, a baroque table lamp with a yellow silk shade and pear-shaped crimson glass base makes a magical focal point on a thrift-shop side table. In an alternative setting, also in New York, floor lamps with quirky Victorian black stands and simple parchment shades present mellow ambient options in a dining area and bedroom.

In general, ancient lighting is low-tech and decorative. It provides few opportunities for accent, task, and information lighting, and therefore works well in conjunction with a modern system. However, one option for old task lighting is ex-commercial lights – former office, surgical, or film lights, for example. A row of ex-office gooseneck lamps mounted above a kitchen work-surface in a Victorian apartment in London is a practical reuse of a design classic. In Jonathan Leitersdorf's New York loft, a row of chrome gooseneck lamps stored on top of a cabinet, awaiting use elsewhere, makes an unusually decorative display.

For performance, efficiency, and design, modern fixtures work well in all four categories of lighting and are a practical, adaptable, and often exhilarating option for all kinds of architectural styles. Unobtrusive recess lights, track lights, and bare-wire lighting (parallel bare wires with miniature spotlights fixed onto, or hanging off, the wires) are good options for ambient lighting. Big-impact contemporary designs make exciting features in ancient and modern interiors. Examples include a mass of bare bulbs jangling from a fan of fine wires in a Victorian living room, and oversize woven paper drums in a converted factory with bare brick walls. Sculptural plastic shapes, glass tubes, and paper globes, which glow or radiate an even light, enliven a space and provide useful satellite lighting on either the floor or low tables. They also create dynamic juxtapositions with ancient structures, surfaces, and elements. Many contemporary floor lamps are wonderful architectural objects in their own right and are ideal for task lighting—for example, as reading lights.

If you prefer low-level light, possibly because it is in keeping with the original intention or historic style of a space (or simply for variation) install dimmer switches or controls as standard with all fixtures.

There are many different ways to adapt antique fixtures. An oil lamp or candle-holding chandelier can be rewired to work on electricity, for example, and there are many different ways to update or extend existing systems. If you have any concerns about the safety of a light or a system, or if you need advice about updating a system, ask an electrician. To find out about new designs and systems, visit a lighting showroom; some offer a free design service.

RIGHT A clip-on spotlight above a mirror is a low-tech solution for essential task lighting in a bathroom.
FAR RIGHT A contemporary "Jack" light by Tom Dixon adds a graphic form as well as variation in lighting to a New York loft.
BELOW In keeping with a new direction in lighting design characterized by simple shapes in white glass or opaque plastic, this globe is a key accent light in a simple bedroom.
BELOW RIGHT Japanese paper lanterns come in all shapes and sizes, from collectable Noguchi originals to inexpensive alternatives, available at department stores. This one is in a former spice factory in New York.

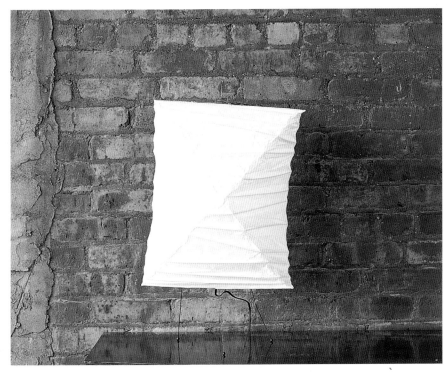

Fixtures and hardware

By definition, fixtures and hardware, such as kitchen sinks, bathtubs, kitchen and bathroom faucets, light switches, door handles, radiators, and built-in shelving, are permanent integral details within a space, essential to how your home looks, feels, and functions. This applies whether you want to leave in place or restore original fixtures, such as a cast-iron rolltop bathtub; use architectural salvage fixtures from the same or a different period of architecture, such as cast-iron radiators; or find contemporary alternatives, like stainless-steel laboratory faucets.

Original storage fixtures are always a bonus, especially an understair cupboard or kitchen pantry that does not extend into valuable living space. Wooden built-in shelves or cabinets provide low-key structural storage solutions that are as visually appealing as they are efficient, and may have had so many coats of paint that they have become conjoined to the surrounding architectural structure. If you are putting in new shelving, it is worth using seasoned wood to avoid cracks and splits. If you plan to leave the wood bare, weathered or bleached boards fit in well with any style of architecture. Choose low-key support brackets or frames to keep the focus on the patina and texture of the wood and on any connection or juxtaposition with the structure of the space.

Changing handles on doors and cabinets, such as introducing tubular aluminum D handles, is a simple way to update a space. As you are likely to be replacing ancient with modern, and not vice versa,

remove just one handle as a tester and check alternatives before you commit to changing all of them. The worn smoothness of a wooden handle on a kitchen cabinet may take some giving up!

If you inherit antique plumbing fixtures like cast-iron radiators, you can use them to create a classic juxtaposition with a contemporary structural element or piece of furniture—a concrete floor, for example, or a glass and metal dining table. Antique or salvaged plumbing adds a sense of history to an interior and often has an appealing chunky design. Mixing ancient and modern plumbing fixtures is relatively easy since pipe sizes are generally standardized. Even if there is a mismatch with pipe or drain sizes, it is usually possible to work around any incompatibility, so you can install any style of radiator, sink, bathtub, or faucets. It is always important to check for signs of erosion. If you buy salvaged plumbing fixtures, do so on the condition that you can swap them if they don't work.

The appeal of salvaged or antique faucets is their worn, smooth surfaces. However, make sure you choose faucets in proportion to the size of your sink, basin, or bathtub—some oversize antique designs overpower modern bath- or kitchenware. In general, decorative faucets look great in bathing areas; utility versions work well in kitchen areas. Juxtaposition between different fixtures, such as a traditional ceramic kitchen sink with a plain modern faucet, avoids predictable period styling and delivers high-tech efficiency to a hard-working area.

LEFT Everything for this low-tech kitchen sink unit was found or bought locally—for example, the wood for the draining board was found in the barn.
RIGHT The industrial look of a stainless-steel commercial stove makes it an ideal stand-alone piece of kitchen equipment. To avoid a cluttered kitchen, choose a design with a built-in backsplash and shelf to store cooking oils.

Antique or salvaged plumbing adds a sense of history to an interior and often has an appealing chunky design.

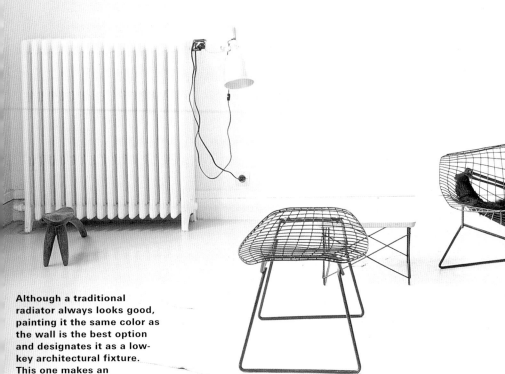

Although a traditional radiator always looks good, painting it the same color as the wall is the best option and designates it as a low-key architectural fixture. This one makes an alternative light stand.

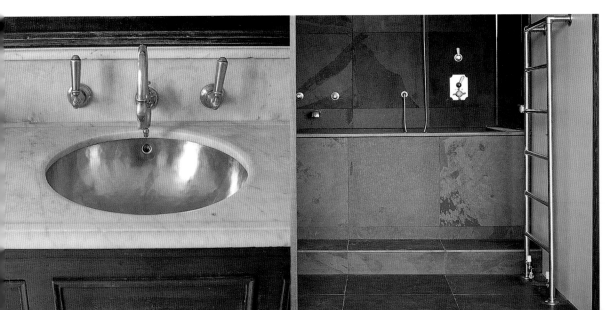

LEFT Natural materials like blue-gray uneven slate tiles and wood and paper shoji screens offset shining chrome bathroom fixtures. FAR LEFT This swan's-head faucet is antique, yet the hot and cold handles are part of a new system. It is usually possible to find a way to combine the aesthetics of antique fixtures with the efficiency and performance of modern ones.

Collection and display

PERSONALIZING A SPLIT-LEVEL APARTMENT WITH A MIX OF FURNITURE AND DETAILS

LEFT Textiles in natural dyes, contemporary tube lighting, and ethnic objects in raw wood contribute shape, color, and meaning to the space.
BELOW LEFT Once used as a container for goat's milk, this African bowl is a compelling central detail in the apartment.
OPPOSITE A simple painted pine table, found in a dumpster and previously used for dining, is now used for display. A friend's sculpture and a china hare reflect the owner's passion for combining the simple with the baroque.

This split-level Art Deco apartment is on the top floor of a 1920s apartment building in Paris, originally designed to provide living and working spaces for artists. Although the apartment is compact, the interior is well planned, organized to perfection, and full of light. White walls, painted concrete floors, and minimal architectural detailing provide a strong, clean backdrop for individual elements and objects that have meaning for and give enjoyment to the style forecaster Gert van de Keuken who lives here.

The economical configuration of the space includes a double-height studio. This has a wall of windows, and these—and the view—are the first things you see when you enter the apartment. They are an important architectural feature with access to a terrace and provide a source of light powerful enough to even out any day-to-day scuffs so that the interior looks positively pristine.

The studio occupies approximately two-thirds of the space and is the main living area. It also provides essential access to the upper level. Various groups of furniture focus on different activities. For example, modern black iron chairs by Harry Bertoia standing on the white-painted reverse side of a cowhide provide a more formal seating area than a bench almost hidden under the stairs with sheepskins on a base of felt pads and colorful cushions made from Moroccan fabrics. Between the windows and the stairs, there is a traditional desk with papers and correspondence, and a flea-market table and two facing chairs stand by the door toward the back of the studio. The shape and orientation of the space mean there is the freedom to organize and use it in many different ways, and without seeming contrived or leaving an obvious passageway these focus groups of furniture allow easy movement through the studio.

At the back of the space, on the lower level, there are a bedroom, bathroom, and dressing room separated from the studio by folding doors with glass panels. Open stairs lead to the eating area on the upper level. In part an open terrace with a balcony like an internal bay window, it overlooks the studio and has a view through the windows. This is very different from the view at the lower level: There is more sky and less intrusion from nearby buildings. The dining table is a wooden workbench that was found in the street. Equally narrow benches from a flea market and Thonet chairs, originally designed in the late 1850s, provide seating. Behind a wall, the adjoining kitchen extends the full width of the space.

Unlike some apartments in the building where the terrace is enclosed to make a bedroom, this one retains its original open-plan structure and a sense of connection between the terrace and the main studio.

Just as it is the nature of this space to be visible and open, any elements or details within it are easy to see and accessible. Part of the enjoyment of the objects on display is their cultural diversity—they include an African goat's-milk bowl, an English painting, and a Japanese pot. Chosen for their shapes and what they mean to the owner and placed by instinct, nothing seems overworked or academic. The objects are not necessarily valuable, yet they reveal the love and appreciation of the person who brought them together.

Ancient and modern ethnic details—especially from Morocco and Africa—are important. Taking an object away from the culture that created it and contrasting it with contemporary architecture focuses attention on the piece: a Moroccan tea table, scraps of felt made into a bedcover, an African milking stool, or a wooden figure. Equally, finding a twig sculpture in a street market in Paris and mixing it with a piece of modern Jean Cocteau pottery creates a refreshing contrast.

Even accidental and everyday combinations—a table set with Japanese ceramic beakers and Swedish dinner plates, for example— make as vital and pleasurable a contribution to the interior as a display of a beach pebble and a piece of sculpture on a pine table. The open-plan arrangement of the space and the blank canvas it provides create the opportunity to put together compositions or accidental groupings of objects, textiles, and lighting on a relatively large scale.

THIS PAGE The simple structure of white walls and a beige-painted concrete floor provides a strong backdrop to an individual collection of furniture, art, artifacts, and textiles. Despite a sense of order, the juxtaposition and arrangement of details add casualness. The owner rarely moves things once he has put them down.

OPPOSITE LEFT Making good use of a semiconcealed space under the stairs, a new built-in bench provides a base for a homemade daybed with soft sheepskins on top of felt pads and pillows made from Moroccan fabrics. The round tables are also from Morocco.

OPPOSITE RIGHT Mixing the colors and shapes of secondhand and contemporary elements, this table setting illustrates the owner's joy and natural ease in putting different objects together.

RESOURCES

Contributors

The following is a list of those whose work was photographed for this book or who supplied products for photography.

ARCHITECTS AND ARCHITECTURAL DESIGNERS

Frederic Mechiche
4 Rue de Thorigny
75003 Paris
France
Tel: 0033 1 4278 7828

J. F. Delsalle
3 Rue Seguier
75006 Paris
France
Tel: 0033 1 4329 4276

Jonathan Leitersdorf
Just Design Ltd
80 Fifth Avenue
18th Floor
New York, NY 10011
Tel: 212 243 6544

Pierre D'Avoine Architects
6A Orde Hall Street
London WC1 N3JW
Tel: 011 (44) 207 242 2124

Smith-Miller + Hawkinson
Architects LLP
305 Canal Street
4th Floor
New York, NY 10013
Tel: 212 966 3875

Stephen Roberts Inc.
270 Lafayette Street
New York, NY 10012
Tel: 212 966 6930

Stickland Combe Architecture
258 Lavender Hill
London SW11 1LJ
Tel: 011 (44) 207 924 1699

Ushida Findlay (UK) Ltd
94 Leonard Street
London EC2A 4RH
Tel: 011 (44) 207 613 4972

ARTISTS

Elena Colombo, sculptor,
New York
Tel: 212 334 5069

Ben Langlands and Nikki Bell,
artists, UK
Tel/Fax: 011 (44) 207 375 2132

Rupert Spira, ceramicist, UK
Tel: 011 (44) 1588 650 588

PRODUCT SUPPLIERS

Michael Benevento
515 Broadway
New York, NY 10012
Tel: 212 965 8617
1940s and 1950s furniture by Le Corbusier, Jean Prouvé, Charlotte Perriand, and Pierre Jeanneret.

The Dining Room Shop
62–64 White Hart Lane
London SW13 0PZ
Tel: 011 (44) 208 878 1020
Extensive selection of antique tables, chairs, and tableware.

Totem Design Group LLC
71 Franklin Street
New York, NY 10013
Tel: 212 925 5506
Contemporary furniture, lighting, textiles, and accessories.

Architects

Brian Murphy
BAM
150 West Channel
Santa Monica, CA 90402
Tel: 310 459 0955

Fernlund and Logan
414 Broadway
New York, NY 10013
Tel: 212 925 9628

Hirst Pacific
250 Lafayette Street
New York, NY 10012
Tel: 212 625 3670

Lot/ek
55 Little West 12th Street
New York, NY 10014
Tel: 212 255 9326

Marino + Giolito
161 West 16th Street
New York, NY 10011
Tel: 212 260 8142

Steve Learner Studio
307 Seventh Avenue
New York, NY10001
Tel: 212 741 8583

Winka Dubbeldam
Archi-tectonics
111 Mercer Street
2nd floor
New York, NY 10012
Tel: 212 226 0303

Advice

Allied Board of Trade
200 Business Park Drive
Armonk, NY 10504
Tel: 914 273 2333
Publishers of the National Directory of Professional Interior Designers and Decorators

The American Institute of Architects
1735 New York Avenue NW
Washington, DC 20006
Tel: 202 626 7300
www.aiaonline.com
Provides guidance on finding and commissioning an architect.

American Society of Interior Designers
608 Massachusetts Avenue NE
Washington, DC 20002
Tel: 202 546 3480

International Interior Design Association
341 Merchandise Mart
Chicago, IL 60654
Tel: 312 467 1960

Retailers and Suppliers

The following is a selection of retailers and suppliers of a wide range of products appropriate for an ancient and modern interior. If you are planning to make a big investment, set a realistic budget and visit showrooms, manufacturers, independent designers, or dealers to see what is available. Check with suppliers for information about nationwide retailers, mail order, and Web sites. If you are looking for a specific ancient, modern, or recycled piece, try to remain open to alternatives. Auctions are a good source of antique items and modern collectible pieces, although it is advisable to check with a specialist or dealer before making a big investment. It is also worth visiting antiques fairs, flea markets, and thrift shops for ancient items.

FLOORING

Acadian Board Company
Tel: 727 393 9668
Manufacturers of recycled DuraCane and other fiberboards, for laminate flooring, furniture, and cabinets.

American Cork Products Company Ltd
Tel: 888 955 2675
Imports more than 30 patterns, colors, and surfaces of cork floor.

Ann Sacks Tile & Stone
115 Steward Street
Seattle, WA 98101
Tel: 800 278 8453 or
503 281 7757
For tiles, stone, and bathtubs.

Bisazza North America
12 West 23 Street, 3rd Floor
New York, NY 10010
Tel: 212 463 0624
Mosaic and glass terrazzo tiles.

Great Harbor Design Center LLC
Brooklyn Navy Yard
Building 12
65 Flushing Avenue
Brooklyn, NY 11205
Tel: 718 596 5829
Suppliers of Icestone—83 percent recycled glass, 17 percent cement—for use as tiling, countertops, etc.

Southern Wood Floors
1 Flowing Wells Road, 472A
Augusta, GA 30907
Tel: 888 488 7463
Reclaimed beams and wood from eighteenth- and nineteenth-century structures, for floors, walls, and cabinetry.

Stone Source
Tel: 212 979 6400 for customer information
Suppliers of stone tiles.

FURNITURE

Aero
Tel: 212 966 1500 for store locations
Contemporary furniture, lighting, and accessories.

Anthropologie
Tel: 212 564 2313 for store locations
Eclectic mix of old and antique furniture including chests, chairs, and tables.

B&B Italia
150 East 58th Street
New York, NY 10155
Tel: 212 758 4046
Contemporary Italian furniture, storage solutions, and lighting.

Cappellini
102 Wooster Street
New York, NY 10012
Tel: 212 966 0669
*International contemporary
furniture collection.*

Cassina
155 East 56th Street
New York, NY 10022
Tel: 212 245 2121
*Contemporary European
furniture and lighting.*

C.I.T.E.
100 Wooster Street
New York, NY 10012
Tel: 212 431 7272
*Former commercial equipment,
including metal cabinets, office
chairs, and lighting.*

Domus Design Collection
181 Madison Avenue
New York, NY 10016
Tel: 212 685 0800
*Contemporary sculptural chairs
and sofas.*

Ethnic Design
53 North East 40th Street
Miami, FL 33137
Tel: 305 573 8118
*Ancient and modern ethnic
pieces plus contemporary items
in old wood.*

Hold Everything
PO Box 7807
San Francisco, CA 94120-7807
Tel: 800 421 2264
*Complete contemporary storage
– from jewelry boxes to
comprehensive systems.*

Jamson Whyte
47 Wooster Street
New York, NY 10013
Tel: 212 965 9405
*Ancient and contemporary Asian
furniture and accessories.*

Knoll
105 Wooster Street
New York, NY 10012
Tel: 212 343 4000
*Twentieth-century iconic
furniture, includng Mies van der
Rohe's Barcelona daybed.*

Modern Age
102 Wooster Street
New York, NY 10012
Tel: 212 966 0669
*Modern and contemporary
pieces.*

Modernica
555 North Franklin Street
Chicago, IL 60610
Tel: 312 222 1808
Modern iconic furniture.

Wyeth
151 Franklin Street
New York, NY 10013
Tel: 212 925 5278
*Eclectic mix of antique, modern,
and ethnic chairs, tables,
cupboards, and sofas.*

LIGHTING

Flos
200 McKay Road
Huntington Station, NY 11746
Tel: 631 549 2745
*Contemporary lighting and
modern classic designs.*

Isamu Noguchi Foundation
Tel: 718 721 2308
Modern classic paper lamps.

Just Bulbs
936 Broadway
New York, NY 10010
Tel: 212 228 7820
*Every kind of bulb, traditional
and contemporary.*

Lighting Plus
676 Broadway
New York, NY 10012
Tel: 212 979 2000
Architectural lighting.

Luminaire
301 West Superior
Chicago, IL 60610
Tel: 312 664 9582
*Contemporary lighting and
furniture.*

HOUSEWARES AND ACCESSORIES

Broadway Panhandler
477 Broome Street
New York, NY 10013
Tel: 212 966 3434
*Good selection of traditional and
contemporary cookware.*

Historical Materialism
125 Crosby Street
New York, NY 10012
Tel: 212 431 3424
*Old glassware, china, and
tableware.*

Indigo Seas
123 N Robertson Boulevard
Los Angeles, CA 90048
Tel: 310 550 8758
*Accessories and furniture for
relaxed living.*

Lucullus
Chartres Street
New Orleans, LA 70130
Tel: 504 528 9620
*Specialists in antique kitchen
and tableware.*

Oggetti
Tel: 305 576 8014 for retailers
near you
*Modern and contemporary
tableware and accessories.*

Williams-Sonoma
Tel: 800 541 2233 for store
locations
*Classic traditional kitchenware
and tableware.*

KITCHEN FIXTURES AND APPLIANCES

Ego Amenities
74 Montauk Highway
East Hampton, NY 11937
Tel: 516 329 9149
*Ceramic sinks, also traditional
and contemporary bathroom
furniture.*

Bulthaup
Tel: 800 808 2923 for
showrooms and retailers
High-specification kitchens.

Chicago Faucets
Tel: 847 803 5000 for customer
information and suppliers
*Stainless-steel faucets including
laboratory-style designs.*

Franke Consumer Products Inc.
Tel: 800 6236 5771 for retailers
Stainless-steel sinks.

Rais & Wittus Inc.
23 Hack Green Road
Pound Ridge, NY 10576
Tel: 914 764 5679
Woodburning stoves.

Viking
Tel: 888 845 4641 for retailers
*Industrial-style kitchen
appliances.*

BATHROOM FIXTURES AND APPLIANCES

Boffi Soho
31 Greene Street
New York, NY 10013
Tel: 212 431 8282
*High-specification minimal
bathroom furniture.*

Hansgrohe
Tel: 800 719 1000 for customer
information and suppliers.
*High-specification showers and
faucets.*

P. E. Guerrin
21–23 Jane Street
New York, NY 10014
Tel: 212 243 5270
*Antique bath fixtures. Visit by
appointment only.*

Waterworks
Tel: 800 899 6757 for customer
information and suppliers
*Bold designs for bathroom
faucets and other fixtures.*

ARCHITECTURAL SALVAGE

Irreplacable Artifacts
14 Second Avenue
New York, NY 10003
Tel: 212 777 2900
*Architectural detailing, including
fireplaces, paneling, plumbing,
and light fixtures.*

Urban Archaeology
143 Franklin Street
New York, NY 10013
Tel: 212 431 4646
*Salvaged door hardware, tiles,
bathroom fixtures, and lighting.*

ONE-STOP SHOPS

Crate&Barrel
650 Madison Avenue
New York, NY 10022
Tel: 212 308 0011
Tel: 800 323 5461 for locations
of other stores
*Contemporary furniture, good
basic housewares, and storage.*

Garnet Hill
Tel: 800 622 6216 for mail-order
information
*Contemporary and iconic
twentieth-century furniture,
lighting, and accessories.*

Home Depot Design Center
Tel: 800 533 3199 for store
locations
Good selection of basic hardware.

IKEA
1000 Center Drive
Elizabeth, NJ 07202
Tel: 908 289 4488
Tel: 888 225 4532 for store
locations
*Inexpensive contemporary
Scandinavian furniture,
housewares.*

Pottery Barn
2109 Broadway
New York, NY 10023
Tel: 800 922 5507 for store
locations
*Contemporary furniture in good
plain materials, including wood,
and neutral colors.*

INDEX

Jacqui Small

Publisher: Jacqui Small
Project editor: Stuart Cooper
Copy editor: Tessa Clark
Designer: Lawrence Morton
Stylist: Cynthia Inions
Production: Geoff Barlow

Rodale Organic Style Books

Executive Editor: Kathleen DeVanna Fish
Executive Creative Director: Christin Gangi
Art Director: Patricia Field
Project Manager: Christine Bucks
Copy Manager: Nancy N. Bailey
Copy Editor: Sarah Sacks Dunn
Manufacturing Coordinator: Jodi Schaffer

Acknowledgments

Thank you Simon Upton for the wonderful photographs in this book and for your determination to keep to the point and to look for—and celebrate— ancient and modern at every opportunity. Thank you Lawrence Morton for a great design; the way you have used the photographs shows that you like them, too!

Thank you Jacqui Small for commissioning me to work on this project. I am very pleased we worked together. Thank you Stuart Cooper for your vital commitment and input.

My biggest thanks to everyone who let us photograph their home—it was a privilege and a delight—and to everyone we met, for your kindness and support. The homes in this book are a mix. Some are the result of people making a space on their own, some are the result of people working with architects and designers, and some are the homes of architects and designers. Thank you Michael Benevento, Elena Colombo, Richard Ferretti and James Gager, Wendy and Fabian Friedland, Andrea Gentl and Marty Hyers, Alastair Gordon and Barbara de Vries, Gert van de Keuken, Ben Langlands and Nikki Bell, Jonathan Leitersdorf, Frederic Mechiche, Sir Giles and Lady Montagu-Pollock, Rupert and Caroline Spira, Yvonne Sporre, Simon Upton, Alannah Weston, and Greville and Sophie Worthington.